SKILL SHARPENERS
STEAM

Keep Your Child's Academic Skills Sharp

This book belongs to

name

Contents

Full STEAM Ahead!

When you apply **Science**, **Technology**, **Engineering**, **Art**, and **Math** to solve a problem, you are using **STEAM**. You can use a **STEAM** approach when you ask questions, analyze, and form ideas for solutions to real-world problems. There is not one correct answer or solution to any problem. In **STEAM**, all ideas are welcome, and you should feel good about the ideas and solutions you come up with.

You can use what you already know and what you will learn about **Science**, **Technology**, **Engineering**, **Art**, and **Math** to form ideas. **STEAM** is about feeling empathy for those impacted by a problem, being creative, and trying out new ideas for solutions.

 So, let's have fun and go **full STEAM ahead** into solving real-world problems!

General Materials List

- pencil or pen
- markers
- crayons
- colored pencils
- digital device

- computer program or app to create pictures, such as a word processing program
- sheets of paper
- device to record audio sounds
- device that can make sounds
- instant coffee
- paintbrushes
- water
- bowls or cups
- plastic bottle caps and lids
- glue
- tempera paints
- large plastic water bottle
- colored tape
- string
- soil
- scissors
- seeds to plant
- household items that can be repurposed

- device to record a video
- cardboard
- tape
- materials with texture, such as beans, seeds, dry pasta, nuts, string, yarn, twine, sandpaper, foil, carpet swatches, orange peel, fabric, leaves, cotton balls
- available room to decorate
- device to take photographs
- materials to decorate a room, such as duct tape, bright-colored fabric, signs and textures, ramp
- mirror
- pipe cleaners
- bubble wrap
- bicycle, if available
- sparkles or glitter
- tissue paper
- soap
- materials that can be used with water, such as sponges, buckets, a kiddie pool, lemons, bubbles, bath-time crayons, washable finger paints
- stapler
- pompoms
- tri-fold poster board

Read the story. Think about the problems in the story.

Why Can't We Make Music?

During lunch, Sami and Rayshawn talked about how much fun it would be to play an instrument. Sami told Rayshawn about her cousin, Elijah. Elijah's school had a band and a music class. Elijah played the drums. Rayshawn declared that he would be amazing at playing the drums. Then he used his plastic fork and spoon to beat a rhythm on the lunch table. Sami started stomping and clapping. Then she jumped up and began dancing.

This attracted the attention of Ms. Ryan, one of the teachers on lunch duty. She thought the students were acting out because they couldn't wait for recess. She came over and said the students were being too loud and distracting others. "We shouldn't get in trouble for expressing ourselves!" burst Sami. Then she asked Ms. Ryan why there wasn't a music program at their school.

Ms. Ryan explained that a music program costs money and there wasn't any money budgeted for music in their school district. "The school board chose to focus on curriculum areas like math, science, and writing, instead of art and music," said Ms. Ryan. "So the funds for the music and arts programs were cut."

Music Education

Is Music Important?

Answer the items about the story you read.

Skills:

Identify key problems and ideas in a text;

Interpret, analyze, and summarize a problem;

Make connections;

Make inferences;

Produce a creative drawing;

Justify an opinion

1. Describe one problem in the story.

   _____

   _____

2. Do you think it was fair of Ms. Ryan to tell the students to quiet down and stop making music?  ○ yes   ○ no

3. The students do not feel like they can fully express themselves because they cannot make music. Draw a picture of one way you like to express yourself.

   [drawing box]

4. Why do you think the school board chose to keep math, science, and writing instead of the music and arts programs? Explain your thinking.

   _____

   _____

5. Do you think students' creativity should be limited based on how much money a school has or how a school board decides to spend its money? Explain.

   _____

   _____

Music Education

Music Education

Music can be a tool for expressing feelings and creativity. Archaeologists, scientists who study human history, have found simple musical instruments that are 43,000 years old! This is evidence that music has been an important part of people's lives for a long time. Music programs have been decreasing in schools, though. Many schools have to stick to a budget, and they sometimes have to cut programs and clubs, including music programs. But many people believe that music education is just as important as subjects such as math and science.

Learning to read music, play an instrument, and appreciate music are skills on their own. But research shows that music education can help students do better in other subjects, too, including math and science. Learning about music can help students with language and reasoning skills, memory, and recognizing patterns. Students who learn to play an instrument practice coordination, which can help with playing sports, too. And being able to sing, play an instrument, and write music can give people a creative way to express their feelings. Music can even help relieve stress.

Skill Sharpeners: STEAM • EMC 9336 • © Evan-Moor Corp.

So, if music has so many benefits, why do some schools have music programs but others do not? One reason that schools cut music programs is to save money. Many schools have a budget, a specific amount of money to spend on learning materials. Schools also have a goal of helping students learn and do well on tests. Students get tested on certain skills, such as math, reading, and writing. Students at most schools do not get tested for their musical abilities. Schools try to give students opportunities to participate in the arts when there is enough money in their budgets. Everything at a school costs money, though, including the chairs, textbooks, and musical instruments. Sometimes, a school has to make tough choices about what to spend money on and what has to be cut from its curriculum.

This boy is using both hands to play the cello and practice coordination.

A school district has a board of education to decide how money will be spent. Members of a school board are elected by the people in the community. Part of the school board's job is to make decisions about the budget. Often, parents and students in school districts speak in front of the board to ask for money for specific programs. Parents and students who want the board to provide funding for a music program might share examples of how music programs in other school districts are run. People can share their opinions about how a school's money is spent and about whether or not a music program is right for their school.

This parent is asking the school board to support the music education program.

Music
Education
and why it is important

Music Education

Make a Song Storyboard

Stories are often told through music. Cities such as London and New York are famous for having musicals, or stories told through music on a stage.

You will write a song that tells a story through words and pictures. The song should be sung to the tune of a song you like.

What You Need

- storyboard graphic organizer on page 11
- markers, crayons, or colored pencils

What You Do

1. On page 11, brainstorm ideas for your song. Think of an idea for a story you want to tell. Think of songs with tunes that you know well. Use the graphic organizer to write your ideas.

2. On page 12, use the storyboard graphic organizer to draw pictures that help tell the story in your song. Think of the pictures as scenes in a movie. Each picture should show a different scene or part of the story.

3. Then write the lyrics to your song under each picture. The lyrics are the words that will help tell the story. Write the lyrics to the tune of a song of your choice.

4. Show your song storyboard to someone and sing the song to them. Then ask the person to tell you what they think your song was about and how the pictures and lyrics helped them know.

The title of my song is

_____.

Describe how you want people to feel when they hear your song.

_____

_____

_____

_____

_____

_____

_____

Describe how your favorite songs make you feel when you hear them.

_____

_____

_____

_____

_____

_____

_____

Write a word or phrase that tells what your song is about, such as *friendship* or *adventure*.

_____

_____

_____

_____

List the names of three songs with tunes you are familiar with.

Song 1: _____

_____

Song 2: _____

_____

Song 3: _____

_____

Storyboard

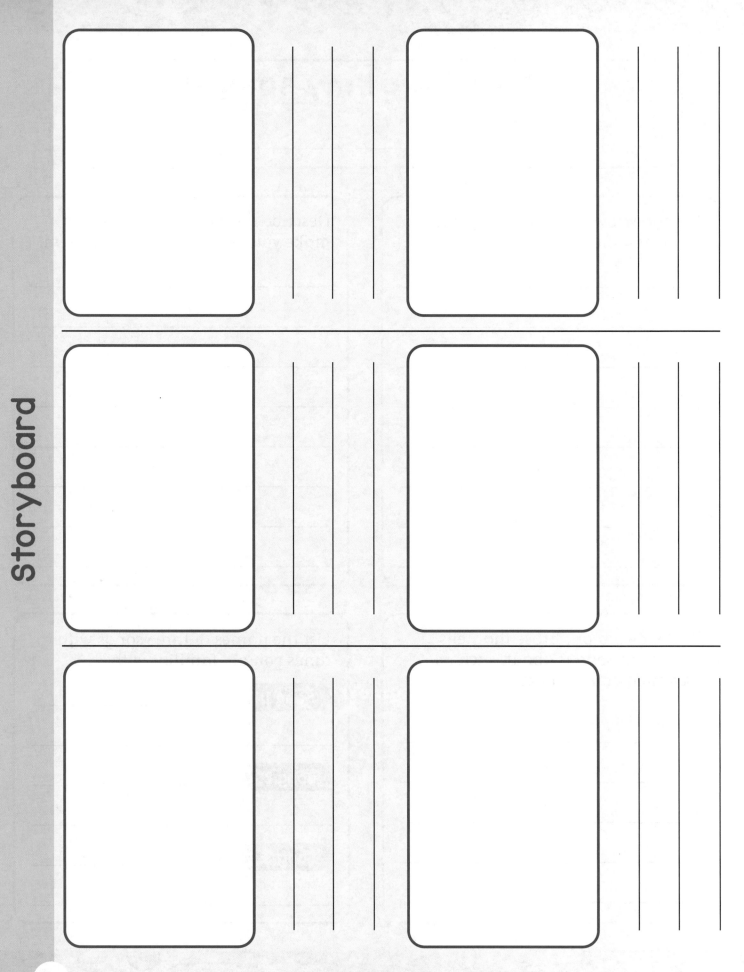

Skill Sharpeners: STEAM • EMC 9336 • © Evan-Moor Corp.

Pitch Perfect

Music has different notes because of how sound waves travel. Learning about sound can help people to better understand music and pitch.

Skills:

Learn about sound waves, pitch, and frequency;

Demonstrate understanding of sound waves;

Make inferences to draw sound waves;

Understand that different musical instruments produce different pitches

When materials vibrate, they send sound waves through the air. We hear these sounds as different pitches, or high and low notes. For a low pitch, the sound waves are low frequency and farther apart. For a high pitch, the sound waves are high frequency and closer together. We can represent sound waves as shown in the diagrams. Use this information to answer the items below.

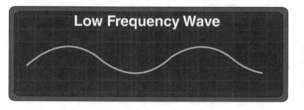

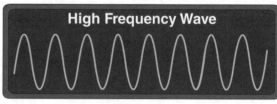

1. Draw the sound waves for the pitch that a flute would make. If you are not sure, find a video of a flute playing or listen to flute music.

2. Draw the sound waves for a pitch that a tuba would make.

3. Draw the sound waves for a pitch that a double bass would make.

Music Education

Feel the Beat!

One of the first things we notice about music is its rhythm, or beat. Music education helps students improve their math skills by experimenting with different rhythms.

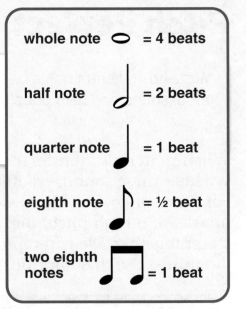

whole note	○	= 4 beats
half note	♩	= 2 beats
quarter note	♩	= 1 beat
eighth note	♪	= ½ beat
two eighth notes	♫	= 1 beat

Music is written in sections called *measures*. Each measure has a certain number of beats, or counts. The chart at the right shows how many beats each written note has.

If a song is written in 4/4 time, each measure has a total of 4 beats. For example, a measure might contain a single whole note, or two half notes, or four quarter notes. The total beats must add up to 4.

1. In 4/4 time, if a measure contains one half note, how many quarter notes can it also contain? _____

   If a measure contains three quarter notes, how many eighth notes can it also contain? _____

2. Clap the following rhythms in 4/4 time (each box is a measure):

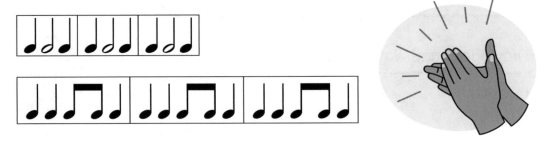

3. Now create your own rhythm and write it below. Write it in measures in 4/4 time. Draw lines to separate the measures.

Music Education

Sound Engineers

Read about the career of sound engineers. Then follow the steps below to practice the skills that sound engineers use.

Skills:
Learn about the career of a sound engineer;

Use a device to practice the skills of sound engineers

Sound engineers are people who work to make music sound a certain way. They work in music recording studios, television studios, and in concert halls. A sound engineer's job is to control the sound levels and outputs so that everything sounds balanced to the audience. If working in a recording studio, the sound engineer is also responsible for editing and mixing the soundtrack. Sound engineers need computer and mechanical skills. They also may have music skills.

1. Use a device to make an audio recording. You can use a computer, phone, tablet, or other device. You can record yourself singing or a song, outdoor nature sounds, or something else.

2. Listen to the recording you made. Then use the device to try to edit the audio recording as much as you can. Try to make the recording sound different from its original version.

3. Listen to the new audio recording that you engineered.

Answer the items.

4. Did you have success in changing the original audio recording to make a new sound? Explain your answer.

_____

_____

5. Do you think you would enjoy being a sound engineer? Explain.

_____

_____

 Music Education

Skills:
Problem solving;
Creative skills;
Solving problem-based, authentic tasks;
Multiple methods;
Multiple content areas;
Connected ideas;
Technology integration

Problem to Solve

The students and parents of Rocky Road Middle School want their school to have a music education program. You will create a presentation for the school board to ask for money for the program.

Task

Read and answer the items on page 17 to research making presentations at school board meetings. Then, on page 18, draft your speech for the presentation and brainstorm ideas for how you can use a digital device in your presentation. Next, give your presentation in front of family or friends. Last, answer the items on page 19.

Rules

- The presentation must include a speech and the use of a digital device that helps show why a music program could benefit the school.

- The speech must mention the purpose of the presentation or what you want the school board to do as a result of the presentation.

- The speech should mention the benefits of music education and explain how music can help students learn many kinds of skills.

- The presentation should be fun and entertaining as well as persuasive.

STEAM Connection

Science	Describe how music education helps with learning other skills.
Technology	Utilize a digital presentation program or device.
Art	Compose an original speech and give a presentation.
Math	Average ratings from other people.

Music Education

Research for Your Presentation

Skills:
Conduct research;
Make observations;
Use visual information;
Hypothesize;
Answer items based on research and observation

Do research to find out more about music programs and school board meetings. Answer the items below.

1. Write a responsibility or concern that school board members have when considering a budget. Then explain how adding a music education program can help address the responsibility or concern.

Responsibility or concern:	How a music program can help:

2. Write how you will use a digital device in your presentation.

_____

3. List the pros and cons of having a school music program. Write at least three in each column.

Pros	Cons

Music Education

Skills:
Use concepts to solve a non-routine problem;

Apply concepts;

Plan a speech and presentation to record;

Create a solution to a problem;

Explain a design

Draft a Speech

Use your answers to the items on page 17 to outline your speech below. On a separate sheet of paper, list digital devices you may use to make the presentation interesting and persuasive.

Write an introduction that tells the purpose of your speech.

_____

_____

Write three important points you want to mention in your speech.

Point 1: _____

_____

Point 2: _____

_____

Point 3: _____

_____

Write a conclusion to the speech that tells what you want the school board to do.

_____

_____

Music Education

Presentation to the School Board

Use a digital device to prepare part of your presentation. Use your speech outline on page 18 to help you write your speech. Then give your presentation to family or friends, as if you are presenting to a school board.

After you are finished, answer the items below.

1. Draw a picture to show what will happen at Rocky Road Middle School if your presentation to the school board is successful.

2. Ask the people who saw your presentation to rate it for each category. Then average their responses for each category and color the stars to show the rating. One star is the lowest rating.

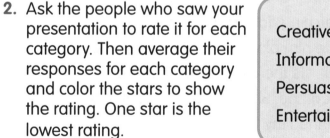

Creative ☆ ☆ ☆ ☆ ☆
Informative ☆ ☆ ☆ ☆ ☆
Persuasive ☆ ☆ ☆ ☆ ☆
Entertaining ☆ ☆ ☆ ☆ ☆

3. Did you like creating a presentation? Write the pros and cons.

Pros	Cons

Music Education

Misinformation

Read the story. Think about the problems in the story.

So Much Information

Zoe and her dad listened to a talk-radio show as he flipped pancakes. The host was interviewing a politician about recent flooding and asked whether rising sea levels were a factor. The politician stated that Earth's sea levels were not changing, and Zoe was confused by this. She saw a graph in science class that showed sea levels have been rising for over a century.

Later, Zoe's friend Monique was listening to a podcast and shared an earbud with Zoe so she could listen, too. The podcast's host was joking about news that people were getting sick from eating at a certain restaurant chain and saying it was because the restaurant workers didn't wash their hands. "Is that even true?" Zoe asked. Monique was laughing too hard to respond, but Zoe was disgusted by what she had heard. She wondered what Monique found so funny. "I don't know if it's true or not, but I'm never eating at that restaurant again," Zoe decided.

After school on Friday, Zoe's older brother, Alex, was watching a vlog on his phone, and Zoe started watching, too. The teenager in the vlog claimed that an energy drink made him play basketball better. Alex told Zoe that he wanted to try the drink. "Is there any proof that a drink can really make you play better?" asked Zoe. She learned in health class that many energy drinks can be unhealthy.

Zoe liked listening to podcasts and watching vlogs. But she was starting to wonder what information was true and what wasn't. "Do the hosts of these shows tell us false information on purpose?" she questioned. It really bothered her that some shows had false information.

Getting the Facts Right

Answer the items about the story you read.

1. Write one problem or conflict that Zoe had with the information being presented in each source she encountered in the story.

Radio show	
Podcast	
Vlog	

2. Zoe decided to never eat at a certain restaurant chain again after hearing information from a podcast. But she wasn't sure if the information was correct. Do you think she made the right decision? Explain your opinion.

_____

_____

3. Who has the bigger responsibility: Should hosts of podcasts, vlogs, and other shows make sure that all the information they state on their show is correct? Or should people make sure they know the facts instead of believing what they hear on shows? Explain your reasoning.

_____

_____

_____

_____

4. In your opinion, what are two of the best sources for true information?

_____   _____

© Evan-Moor Corp. • EMC 9336 • Skill Sharpeners: STEAM

Skills:

Identify key problems and ideas in a text;

Interpret, analyze, and summarize a problem;

Make connections;

Make inferences;

Justify an opinion

Misinformation

Carefully Looking at Our Sources

There are so many choices when it comes to Internet sites, vlogs, podcasts, radio stations, television shows, social media platforms, and news channels. There are hilarious online videos that will make you laugh until your tummy hurts. There are serious articles about environmental issues and true human experiences. Some people are interested in space exploration and technology. Some people are interested in math and sports. You can find sources about bugs, surfing, plants, and other things. Even though there are a lot of sources for information, there is also a lot of misinformation available. Often the things we read, see, and hear in sources are just not true. But there are things we can try to do to be sure we are getting information that is correct.

Why is it important to get correct information? Think about local events that happen in your community. Imagine that you love going to your county fair every year, for example. You may go to the Internet to find the dates the fair will be open. But how would you feel if the dates posted online were wrong, and you ended up missing the fair altogether because of the incorrect information? This is just one example of how misinformation could affect your life. Every single day, millions of people around the world are trying to get information about different topics from many sources. People turn to blogs, vlogs, social media, and other sources to find out about nutrition, voting for the next president, pet care, education, the weather, and so many other important topics. The information we get helps us make choices in our daily lives.

Misinformation

Skill Sharpeners: STEAM • EMC 9336 • © Evan-Moor Corp.

Concepts:

Many media sources present opinions as if they are facts;

There is misinformation as well as accurate information in the media, and it can be challenging sometimes to figure out which information is accurate;

Technology helps to allow more people to post information online for others to see

Podcasts are popular sources of information. A podcast is an audio file, or a sound recording, that you listen to on a digital device. Some podcasts have many installments, or episodes. A podcast may focus on doing interviews, telling fictional stories, or sharing news. Some podcasts are just about one person's opinions on a subject. Pretty much anyone can make a podcast— basically all you need is a smart device or computer that can make audio recordings and upload them to the Internet. It's the same with vlogs, which are short videos that people can post online or on a social media channel. Anyone who has the tools can put information on the Internet for others to receive.

Because there are so many people posting their own websites, podcasts, blogs, and vlogs, there are a lot of opinions instead of facts being shared. Sharing an opinion is not a negative thing. We all have opinions, and all opinions are valid. But one problem that can occur is mistaking people's opinions for facts. And in the media, people sometimes state their opinions as if they are facts, which is how misinformation can spread.

There are things you can do to try to get correct information. Ask yourself some key questions about the sources you are using to get information. Another thing you can do is find out what sources your teachers and parents know and trust.

Key questions to ask about a source:

- [ ] Is the person who created this source an expert in the subject?

- [ ] Does the URL end with one of these: **.org**, **.edu**, or **.gov**? (These types of sites are usually trustworthy.)

- [ ] Has the source been updated recently?

- [ ] Is this source trying to sell you something or convince you to give money?

Misinformation

Art Connection

Skills:

Convey an idea through visual art;

Explore uses of materials and tools to create works of art or design;

Use observation and investigation in preparation for making a work of art;

Demonstrate creativity;

Follow detailed instructions

Design a Podcast Web Page

There are so many different types of podcasts. Some podcasts are funny. Some are about science or history. How can podcast creators advertise and make their shows seem interesting to attract more listeners?

Imagine that you are a web page designer. You have a customer who is the host of a podcast. Your job is to design a web page for the podcast. There will be a new episode each week, and each episode will be 30 minutes long. The topic of the podcast is "Foods from Different Cultures."

What You Need

- any computer program you can use to create pictures, such as a word processing program (if available)
- paper
- crayons, markers, or colored pencils

What You Do

1. Look at some websites to get an idea for how you want your web page to look. Use the items on page 25 to help plan the web page. Consider the topic of the podcast you are designing your web page for.

2. Plan the following features to include on your artistic web page:
   - the name of the podcast;
   - images such as photos, maps, symbols, and illustrations;
   - at least three links (or text that just looks like a link); and
   - at least two drop-down menu options to click on.

3. On page 26, sketch out a rough draft of what your web page will look like. Think about where each feature will go on the page.

4. Now use a computer program or other materials to create your web page for a podcast about foods from different cultures. If possible, print the page when you're finished making it.

Misinformation

24

Answer the items below to help plan your web page.

1. What colors will you use on your web page? List them.

_____   _____   _____

_____   _____   _____

2. Websites often have an easy-to-remember URL. Think of a catchy or interesting URL to use for your website. Write it below.

3. Think about the words that will appear on the web page. Write words you can use for links or drop-down menus.

_____   _____   _____

_____   _____   _____

Sketch your web page.

Sound Technology

Skills:

Compare and contrast analog and digital recordings;

Recognize analog and digital recordings in the real world

Pretty much anyone who has a recording device and access to the Internet can make their own podcast. When someone makes a podcast, sound must be recorded. There are different formats for recording sound—analog and digital. Most recordings today use digital recording.

An analog recording is an electronic copy of an original sound, such as someone talking or singing. The sound waves are converted into electrical signals and stored on some type of medium, such as a tape or vinyl album. A digital recording converts the sound waves into a stream of numbers. When we want to listen to a digital recording, the numbers get converted back into sound waves. Smart phones and CDs use digital audio technology.

1. Use the Venn diagram to compare and contrast analog and digital recordings. Write one thing in each part of the diagram.

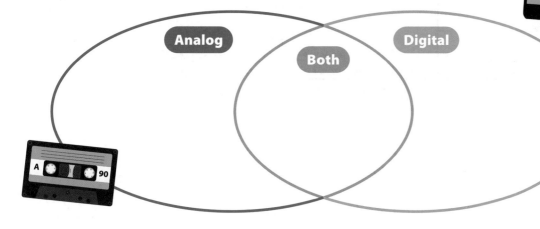

Analog   Both   Digital

2. Which of the following types of media have you used to listen to music?

- ○ vinyl record
- ○ CD
- ○ radio
- ○ cassette tape
- ○ smartphone
- ○ other music app
- ○ website
- ○ MP3 player
- ○ television

3. Do you prefer analog or digital recordings?

_____

Misinformation

Analyzing Podcast Programs

Podcasts have become increasingly popular over the past decade, and more and more people of all ages are turning to podcast programs for information and entertainment.

Study the bar graph and answer the items.

Podcasts People Are Listening To

(Bar graph with y-axis from 0% to 100% in 20% increments; categories: talk shows, news and current affairs, comedy, storytelling, sports)

1. Which category has the most listeners? _____

   What percentage of the total listeners is this? _____

2. Which category has the fewest listeners? _____

   What percentage of the total listeners is this? _____

3. Based on the data, why is it important for podcasts to contain factual information?

   _____

   _____

Skills:

Read a bar graph;

Use data presented in a bar graph to answer questions;

Calculate percentages;

Practice mathematical reasoning

Misinformation

Podcast Editors

After a podcast is recorded, it usually needs some editing. Editing involves cutting out parts of the recording and changing the recording. Parts are cut or changed when they are unclear or have mistakes and unwanted noises, such as coughs and sneezes. Sometimes, podcast editors add sound effects or music. A podcast editor has an important role in making sure that the podcast is accurate and doesn't have misinformation. Sometimes, the host or creator of the podcast is the same person who edits it.

Skills:

Learn about the career of a podcast editor;

Formulate and justify an opinion;

Consider the skills of podcast editors;

Make inferences

1. What is the biggest responsibility of a podcast editor: to make sure that the podcast is entertaining or to make sure there is no misinformation? Explain your opinion.

   _____

   _____

   _____

2. What are some skills that a podcast editor must have? Fill in the circles next to any you think are important.

   ○ athletic skill   ○ creativity   ○ attention to detail

   ○ computer skills   ○ writing skills   ○ technology skills

3. Is podcast editing something you think you would enjoy? Explain why or why not.

   _____

   _____

   _____

Misinformation

Problem to Solve

Skills:

Problem solving;

Creative skills;

Solving problem-based, authentic tasks;

Multiple methods;

Multiple content areas;

Connected ideas;

Technology integration

People in your community are disagreeing about an issue. Many people support cutting down trees in the forest to create a mall, which will create jobs and bring in more shops and restaurants. But other people think it's more important to preserve the wildlife and natural forest. You will create a podcast episode to inform the community about the issue.

Task

Read and answer the items on page 31 to research the topic of your podcast. Then, on page 32, write a script for your podcast. Next, record your podcast. Last, answer the items on page 33.

Rules

- The recording can have you speaking alone or include other people talking.

- The recording should model a podcast and be entertaining and informative.

- The podcast must include at least one sound effect or music.

STEAM Connection

Science	Research a science topic.
Technology	Use a device to make an audio recording.
Engineering	Design and create a recording.
Art	Create an entertaining and informative recording that models a podcast.

Misinformation

Skill Sharpeners: STEAM • EMC 9336 • © Evan-Moor Corp.

Research the Podcast's Topic

Skills:

Conduct research;

Make observations;

Use visual information;

Hypothesize;

Answer items based on research and observation

Do research to find out more about podcasts and habitat loss. Answer the items below to help you plan your podcast on page 32.

1. Write two additional pros and two additional cons (ones not mentioned on page 30) to cutting down part of the forest to build a mall.

Pros	Cons

2. What is your opinion on this issue? Explain why.

_____

_____

3. Will you include your opinion in your podcast episode?   ◯ yes   ◯ no

4. Listen to a podcast episode, a vlog, or another type of media. Then write two ideas that this gives you for making your own podcast recording.

Idea 1: _____

Idea 2: _____

5. Draw and label devices you can use to create your podcast.

[ ]   [ ]   [ ]

_____   _____   _____

Misinformation

Outline the Podcast

Write in the spaces below to outline ideas to bring up while recording your podcast. A podcast usually sounds like a casual conversation rather than a formal presentation, so you do not have to write everything that you or others plan to say. You will use this outline as you record.

Skills:

Use concepts to solve a non-routine problem;

Apply concepts;

Write a script to use while recording a podcast;

Create a solution to a problem;

Explain a design

Write what you will say to introduce yourself and the podcast. Include the podcast episode's title.

Plan and describe the sound effect(s) or music you will use.

Write three things you want to bring up during the recording.

Write what you will say to end the podcast recording.

Misinformation

Record the Podcast

Use the outline you created to record your podcast with sound effects or music. After you finish recording, answer the items below.

Skills:
Create a podcast recording;

Reflect on the recording you created;

Compare and contrast the podcast recording you created to other podcast recordings;

Formulate and justify an opinion;

Practice self-awareness

1. Listen to your podcast recording. Then write two things you like about it and two things you would change.

Things I like	Things I would change
1. _____	1. _____
2. _____	2. _____

2. Do you listen to any real-world podcasts? If yes, explain how the recording you made compares to ones you've listened to. If no, explain whether or not you would listen to a podcast like the one you created and why.

_____

_____

_____

3. What is your opinion about podcasts and other forms of media that have misinformation? Do you think this is an important problem that needs to be addressed? Explain your opinion.

_____

_____

_____

Misinformation

Repurpose Items

Read the story. Think about the problems in the story.

A Day in Khean's Life

Khean should have been excited. The Angkor Warriors were playing that evening. Unfortunately, he had no way to watch the televised soccer match. "Oh well," he thought. "I'll hear about it tomorrow."

Right now, Khean had work to do. He put on his one pair of shorts and went outside. Drawing water from a plastic jug, he cleaned his teeth with a stick and baking soda. Next, he waded out into the river, where he saw his frustrated father struggling with a fishing net. "This net had a hole," Khean's father said. "It took fifteen minutes to mend it. Help me lay it in the water." Khean did as he was told.

It was a long day for Khean and his dad, but, luckily, it was a good fishing day. In the late afternoon, they carried laundry hampers out to the net and filled them with fish. They sold most of the fish at the market. Then they bought some rice and vegetables. Khean's stomach grumbled as he looked at the small amount of food they'd have for dinner. There was some money left, but Khean knew they'd need to save it in case someone in his family got sick and needed medicine.

Back home, Khean's mother cooked over a small fire in the yard. After dinner, Khean was tired. But his mother had a surprise. "We're going to the neighbor's to watch the soccer match," she said. Everyone in the village gathered around an old television set. It was powered by a car battery. The picture was a little grainy, but that didn't matter to Khean.

Using What Is Available

Skills:
Identify key problems and ideas in a text;

Interpret, analyze, and summarize a problem;

Make connections;

Make inferences;

Produce a creative drawing;

Justify an opinion

Answer the items about the story you read.

1. What is the biggest problem in the story?

   _____

   _____

2. Write one thing that you think Khean would have more of if he could.

   _____

3. Compare Khean's life with yours. Write one thing in each part of the Venn diagram.

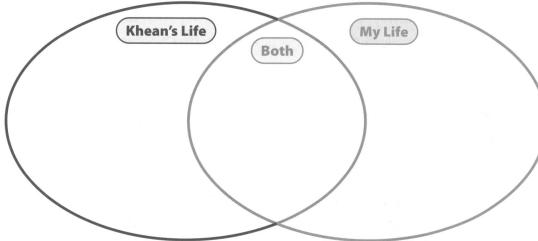

Khean's Life   Both   My Life

4. The people in the story repurposed some objects by using them for different purposes than what they were meant for. Are there any objects that you or your family has repurposed? Write the name of the object. Then draw a picture showing how it was repurposed.

   _____

   _____

Repurpose Items

Repurposing Items

According to the World Bank, the minimum amount of money a person needs to survive is $1.90 per day. A person living on less than that is considered to be living in extreme poverty. Over 700 million people live in extreme poverty. That's about 10% of the world's population. There's poverty all over the world and on every continent. And millions of other people who are not living in extreme poverty may have difficulty getting things they need to live. Not everyone can afford to buy new items frequently. Repurposing items can help anyone who is trying to save money and get the most use out of objects.

People need money to meet their basic needs, such as getting food, clean water, shelter, clothing, and healthcare. Many people want to save money and avoid wasting or adding to landfills. They will try to make items useful for as long as possible by reusing, repairing, and repurposing them.

Not all items have to be thrown away when they get old or break. For example, if your shoe's sole is starting to come apart, you can use strong glue to fix it and make the shoe wearable again. Old mugs can be repurposed as planters.

Egg carton repurposed as a planter

Grow your own ☺ Vegetables

Repurpose Items

A squeezable ketchup bottle doesn't need to go into the recycling bin. It can be washed out and used to squirt pancake batter into a pan. Old worn out clothing can be cut into pieces and used as rags for cleaning. Old clothing can also be cut and sewn into cloth bags. Broken pieces of crayons can be turned into candles by being melted and poured into a jar with a wick.

There are also alternatives to the cleaning solutions people buy from stores. For example, items such as vinegar and baking soda can be used for cleaning countertops and other surfaces in a home. Baking soda can help remove stains and odors. Many people also combine baking soda and coconut oil and use the mixture as toothpaste. Lemon juice can also be used to clean and help a kitchen smell nice. A family could save money by using homemade cleaning solutions.

There are a lot of creative ways to repurpose things, and repurposing can also be good for the environment. It results in less trash ending up in landfills. And consider the fact that many items get thrown away when they are still in usable condition. Imagine all of the repurposing possibilities the next time you are thinking of throwing away something that could still be useful!

Concepts:

Many people live in extreme poverty;

A lot of people try to save money by repurposing items or making homemade items;

DIY projects are common;

Many people find creative ways to repurpose items

Repurpose Items

Wood pallets repurposed as an outdoor table and chairs

Repurposed Art

You can reuse or repurpose items and make beautiful artwork. Here are three projects that repurpose things you might find in your house.

Project 1: Coffee Art

Coffee can be used just like watercolor paints. Instant coffee is generally considered to be affordable, so it is a handy medium for creating artwork.

What You Need

- instant coffee
- sheet of paper
- pencil
- paintbrushes
- water
- 3 bowls or cups

What You Do

1. On a sheet of paper, sketch a picture that you will paint over.

2. In each bowl or cup, create a different mixture of coffee and water. Create a thick one with a lot of instant coffee. Create a thin one with less coffee and one with a medium thickness. The thicker the mixture, the darker the paint will be on the page.

3. Use the paintbrushes and mixtures to paint over the picture you sketched. Use all three mixtures to create different shades of color. You can also add more layers of the mixtures for an extra dark shade.

4. After you finish painting, let your artwork dry. Then hang it up to enjoy!

Repurpose Items

Project 2: Bottle Cap Collage

Plastic bottle caps and lids come in different colors and sizes, and they usually can't be recycled. Instead of sending them to a landfill, turn them into an eye-catching piece of art.

What You Need

- bottle caps and lids
- pencil
- large sheet of paper
- glue
- tempera paints
- paintbrush

What You Do

1. Collect as many bottle caps and lids as you can. Any other small pieces of plastic can be used as well. Sort them by colors.

2. Draw a sketch to plan your design. Decide which colors certain areas of your picture will be.

3. Glue the bottle caps and lids onto the paper to create your art.

4. If you don't have enough bottle caps and lids to cover the entire paper, that's okay. You can use paint to fill the empty areas.

5. Hang up your artwork for everyone to see.

Repurpose Items

Project 3: Plastic Bottle Planter

Plastic water bottles make great planters. When you repurpose a water bottle to make a planter, you're not just giving new life to that bottle— you're bringing new plant life to the planet.

What You Need

- large plastic water bottle
- paint or colored tape
- utility knife or scissors
- string
- soil
- vegetable, flower, or herb seeds

What You Do

1. Have an adult use a utility knife or scissors to cut off the top of the bottle. Then poke a hole through the bottle, just below the edge where it was cut. Poke another hole directly across from the first hole.

2. Cut a long piece of string. Thread the string through both of the holes and tie it at the top.

3. Use paint or colored tape to make a design on your planter. Decorate it any way you'd like.

4. Fill the planter with soil.

5. Plant a few seeds in the soil. Lightly water it.

6. Hang your planter somewhere with plenty of sunlight and remember to water it!

Repurpose Items

Skill Sharpeners: STEAM • EMC 9336 • © Evan-Moor Corp.

Reusing and Repurposing

People can repurpose items and use them for new things. This can help people save money and avoid being wasteful. We can also make things that are useful out of natural materials. For example, we use cornstalks to make scarecrows, which help scare away pests from crops.

Look at the photos. Draw an **X** beside each one that shows something being repurposed.

In some places, coconuts grow naturally and are plentiful. Coconut shells can be used to make bowls. Think of another way that a coconut shell could be changed or used by people. Write it below.

Repurposed Objects

Many things are designed for a specific purpose. But a lot of objects can be repurposed and used for different tasks. Many people are creative with their uses of objects!

Look at the photos. Then answer the items.

1. Which object could be repurposed and used to create a goal area for a soccer game? Explain your thinking.

   _____

   _____

   _____

2. Which object could be repurposed and used as a dish to eat from? Explain your thinking.

   _____

   _____

   _____

Repurpose Items

Being Resourceful

Skills:
Learn about ways people are resourceful;

Use visual information;

Think critically and creatively

People often have to be resourceful and creative. People who are resourceful find clever ways to repurpose items. Teachers often repurpose objects in their classrooms to help them teach. Much of the time, people repurpose items in order to meet their needs. Repurposing items can save money and get the most use out of objects. Look at the photos. Read about how some people use the objects shown. Then write two other ideas for how to use each object.

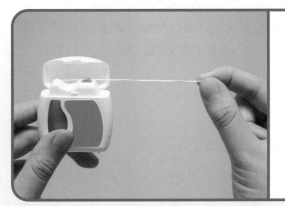

Some people use dental floss to slice foods such as cake or cheese.

Eagle Scouts will sometimes use dental floss instead of thread to sew buttons onto clothing.

Idea 1: _____

Idea 2: _____

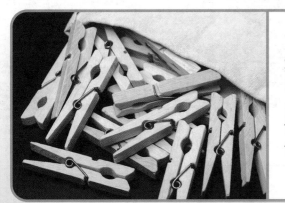

Some people use clothespins in their hair. Teachers use clothespins for art projects. Many people use clothespins for what they were originally designed for—hanging clothes.

Idea 1: _____

Idea 2: _____

Repurpose Items

Problem to Solve

A lot of things people buy in stores can be made from household items. Household items can be repurposed and used for different tasks. You will make a Do-It-Yourself (DIY) video that shows four different things you can either make or repurpose using items in your house.

Task

Answer the items on page 45 to research DIY projects. Then, on page 46, create an outline of which projects you will show and what you will say in your video. Next, make your video. Last, answer the items on page 47.

Rules

- The DIY projects must use a variety of household items that you have available.

- The video should show you making things or using repurposed things for four different purposes or uses.

STEAM Connection

Technology	Use a smartphone or a tablet to make a video.
Engineering	Figure out how things can be repurposed and/or assembled.
Art	Make crafts; create and edit a video.

Repurpose Items

Research Repurposing Items

Skills:
Conduct research;
Make observations;
Use visual information;
Hypothesize;
Answer items based on research and observation

Research how to repurpose objects. Answer the items below to help you plan your instructional video on page 46.

1. Search for DIY videos on the Internet. Look for ones that show how to make things or repurpose household objects. Write notes below.

   _____

   _____

   _____

2. Items can be repurposed to make something that looks nice. Or they can be repurposed to make something that performs a function. On a scale of 1 to 10, indicate how important each quality is to you.

   looks nice

   ① ② ③ ④ ⑤ ⑥ ⑦ ⑧ ⑨ ⑩

   performs a function

   ① ② ③ ④ ⑤ ⑥ ⑦ ⑧ ⑨ ⑩

3. The items below can be repurposed and used to make something else. Fill in the circle beside the items you have in your house. Then write additional items you could use.

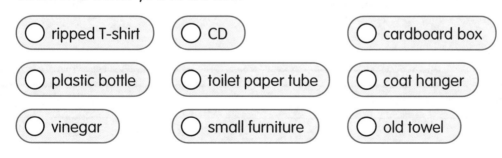

   ○ ripped T-shirt   ○ CD   ○ cardboard box

   ○ plastic bottle   ○ toilet paper tube   ○ coat hanger

   ○ vinegar   ○ small furniture   ○ old towel

   _____   _____   _____

Repurpose Items

Plan Your Video

Create an outline for your video about DIY projects. Write four projects you will try to make and their materials. Then write one thing you want to say about each project in the video.

Project:	
Materials:	**Statement to say in the video:**

Project:	
Materials:	**Statement to say in the video:**

Project:	
Materials:	**Statement to say in the video:**

Project:	
Materials:	**Statement to say in the video:**

Skills:

Use concepts to solve a non-routine problem;

Apply concepts;

Plan a DIY video;

Create a solution to a problem;

Explain a design

Repurpose Items

Make Your Video

Make your video showing how to make or repurpose four items using household materials.

After you finish recording the video, answer the items below.

Skills:

Create a DIY video;

Evaluate repurposing;

Convey the purpose of the video;

Receive feedback on the video;

Practice self-awareness

1. Show your video to a friend or family member. Then ask him or her the following questions and write the answers:

   Were you able to understand how to do the projects? _____

   Would you make or use any of these things? _____

   What is more important to you: saving money or time? _____

2. Imagine that you're going to post your video on the Internet. Write a brief summary of the video that will make people want to watch it.

   _____

   _____

3. What positive consequences would there be if everyone made their own things? What negative consequences might there be? Write at least two things in each part of the chart.

Positives	Negatives

Repurpose Items

Concepts:

It is common for abilities to change as people get older;

Some older adults choose to live in a place where they can get extra help with their medical needs;

It can be challenging for people to see their loved ones' abilities change as they get older

Making Places Safer

Read the story. Think about the problems in the story.

Grandpa's New Home

Raffi and his mom pulled up at his grandpa's new home. "Grandpa must love this place!" Raffi commented. "He always wanted to live by a forest. I've missed him so much."

"I think he does like it here so far," Raffi's mom said. "There are a lot of other people living in this building who are close to Grandpa's age, and there are nurses to help out, too." Just then, they saw Grandpa approaching.

"Welcome!" he said, reaching out his left arm to give a hug.

"Grandpa, what happened to your arm?" Raffi asked alarmed.

"Well, I took a tumble my first day here," Grandpa explained. "I was entering the dining hall. The flooring is all brown, and I didn't notice that there were gaps between some of the wooden panels. My shoe got caught for a second. I tripped and landed on my wrist. What a great first impression I made on all my new friends," he said, rolling his eyes and smiling.

They all got on an elevator with another resident named Marla. Grandpa introduced Raffi and his mom. "Nice to meet you, and excuse me for not shaking hands," Marla said, nodding at her crutches. "Watch out when you use the laundry room, by the way. They poured a new concrete floor. It's now an inch higher than it was before."

During the visit, Raffi noticed that other residents were using crutches and wearing casts. "Grandpa, is this place safe? I see others with injuries."

"Well, this *is* a senior community," Grandpa reminded him with a chuckle. "For some of us, our eyes aren't as sharp as they used to be. We just have to pay better attention."

Skill Sharpeners: STEAM • EMC 9336 • © Evan-Moor Corp.

Grandpa's Safety

Answer the items about the story you read.

1. Describe two problems in the story.

Problem 1	Problem 2
_____	_____
_____	_____
_____	_____

2. What do you think caused Marla to need crutches? Explain your thinking.

_____

_____

_____

3. Why do you think there are nurses to help out at Grandpa's new home?

_____

_____

4. Write two suggestions for how the building Raffi's grandpa lives in could be changed to make it safer for people who might not be able to see as well as they used to.

Suggestion 1	Suggestion 2
_____	_____
_____	_____
_____	_____

© Evan-Moor Corp. • EMC 9336 • Skill Sharpeners: STEAM

Skills:

Identify key problems and ideas in a text;

Interpret, analyze, and summarize a problem;

Make connections;

Make inferences;

Suggest possible solutions to a problem;

Justify an opinion

Making Places Safer

Making Places Safer

We all want our loved ones to be safe and healthy. Part of being safe is maintaining our homes and environments so that they are not dangerous or harmful to our health. And sometimes our abilities change as we get older. Some of our loved ones who are older need to be in an environment that takes their abilities into consideration.

As people age, their bodies and abilities may start to change. It is important to remember that many people pay attention to their health and remain in great health even as they get older. Still, there are common changes that happen to all people as they age, even to the healthiest people. For example, there are age-related eye conditions that can form, and many people start to suffer some sight loss. A person's bone density can decrease with age as well. This means that the bones become more brittle and less strong. With age, skin may become thinner and more fragile. Many people have less fat directly under their skin when they get older, too. This layer of fat can actually help protect people from injury. As we get older, it's harder to gain muscle, and a lot of people find it harder to bend at their joints. These bodily changes can make it more difficult to move or react quickly. This is why some older adults need help with walking or need eyeglasses, even though they didn't need these things when they were younger.

Changes to people's abilities and bodies can lead to higher chances of them getting injured or suffering a fall.

Evidence shows that there are a lot of people 65 years old and older who fall each year.

Skill Sharpeners: STEAM • EMC 9336 • © Evan-Moor Corp.

The National Council on Aging (NCOA) states that in the United States alone, an older adult is treated in a hospital for a fall about every 11 seconds. The Centers for Disease Control and Prevention (CDC) also states that falls are the leading cause of fatal injury among older adults. Many older adults live in fear of falling, so they limit the activities they enjoy and the places they go to avoid the possibility of falling.

It is important to remember that falls are often preventable. The NCOA claims that simply being older is not going to cause people to fall. It says that practical lifestyle adjustments, or simple changes, can help prevent falls. There are fall-prevention programs that focus on trying to help people learn how they can decrease the chances of themselves and loved ones falling.

Some people fall because of vision difficulties. For people who have trouble seeing clearly, staircases can be dangerous. It can be hard to tell how high each stair step is, how many steps there are, or where the staircase ends and the floor begins. It is even more difficult if there are no bold colors or marks on the stairs or when lighting is dim. When outdoors, it can be difficult to see cracks in a sidewalk or if a sidewalk is uneven. So how can we make surroundings safer for people who are experiencing changes in their abilities or some vision loss? The NCOA has the following suggestions:

- Adjust lighting so it's bright enough to see but not glaring.
- Use contrasting colors and brightly colored designs to make objects and floor changes stand out more boldly.
- Make sure that rugs won't move or catch on a shoe.
- Clean up clutter and obstacles from the floor.

Making some simple changes could help make a place safer for people who need a little help with telling objects apart and avoiding falls.

© Evan-Moor Corp. • EMC 9336 • Skill Sharpeners: STEAM

Making Places Safer

Making Places Safer

Make a Texture "Painting"

Imagine that your community center is holding an art exhibit called Beautiful to the Touch. The exhibit features art for people who are experiencing vision loss. Instead of using paint, all the artists will use materials with texture to create lines, shapes, and contrast.

Create an original work of art. Use at least six different textures.

What You Need

- cardboard
- pencil
- glue or tape
- texture reference sheet on page 53
- variety of materials with texture, such as beans, seeds, dry pasta, nuts, string, yarn, twine, sandpaper, foil, carpet swatches, orange peel, fabric, leaves

What You Do

1. Look at the examples of textures on page 53. Imagine how each texture feels when you touch it. Think about the textures you want to use on your painting.

2. Then, on page 54, sketch the basic shapes or scene you want to "paint." It can be a portrait, a still life, a landscape, or an abstract design.

3. Decide which materials you will use to make different lines, shapes, or patterns.

4. Use the cardboard as your canvas. Use glue or tape to affix the materials. As you work, close your eyes and lightly run your hand over different places in the picture to make sure there is contrast in the textures and that lines and shapes are distinct.

5. Hang your painting, and invite blindfolded family members and friends to touch and enjoy your artwork.

Textures

Look at the examples of textures. Think about other materials that have these textures and what you can use in your artwork. You can use other textures, too.

smooth

rough

hard

soft

woven

bumpy

squishy

ridged

Sketch your picture here. Note the textures you will use in each part of the picture.

Some Vision Loss Conditions

Skills:

Learn about conditions that can result in vision loss;

Use visual information to match photographs with medical conditions;

Make inferences

People with different eye conditions may experience different forms of vision loss:

Macular degeneration makes the shape of objects look crooked or covers objects with a dark smudge.

Glaucoma can cause side vision loss or total side vision blindness.

A **cataract** makes everything look cloudy or blurry.

Look at each photo. Write which condition each photo represents, based on the information provided above.

_____   _____   _____

Explain how each condition could possibly lead to someone falling.

Macular degeneration: _____

_____

Glaucoma: _____

_____

Cataract: _____

_____

Making Places Safer

Making Changes to Spaces

People can customize, or change, the places where they live. Some people repaint rooms different colors, hang items on walls, change doorknobs, and install things such as carpets in their houses. There is no limit to the changes we can make to our living spaces.

The Ochoas retired after their children had all moved out, and they moved to a smaller house. They need help making some changes to their new house to make it safer for them. Look for possible hazards in each room. Write one thing that could be done to make it safer.

1. bathroom

_____

_____

_____

2. dining area

_____

_____

_____

3. kitchen

_____

_____

_____

_____

Making Places Safer

Helping People with Vision Loss

Skills:
Learn about careers that can help people with vision loss and making environments safer;

Make inferences

Read the description of each career professional. Each one can help people with vision loss in a different way. Write one way each person can help.

Career Professional	How he or she can help senior citizens
Optometrist checks eye health and treats some vision conditions	_____ _____ _____ _____
Architect designs homes, offices, and other structures with useful spaces	_____ _____ _____ _____
Interior Designer chooses a home's colors, fabrics, fixtures, and furniture	_____ _____ _____ _____
Occupational Therapist teaches people different ways of doing everyday things	_____ _____ _____ _____

Making Places Safer

Skills:

Problem solving;

Creative skills;

Solving problem-based, authentic tasks;

Multiple methods;

Multiple content areas;

Connected ideas;

Technology integration

Problem to Solve

Your parents have invited an elderly relative to move into your home. You have been asked to examine the areas of your home to look for ways to make it safer. Choose one room to make safer for your relative and take before-and-after photos of it.

Task

Read and answer the items on page 59 to research how areas can be decorated or designed to be safer for people with some vision loss. Then, on page 60, brainstorm changes you plan to make to the room. Take photos of the room before and after making the safety changes. Last, answer the items on page 61.

Rules

- The room you choose should have at least two changes made to it.

- The photos you take should show the room before you changed it and then show the changes you made.

- Materials may include colorful duct tape, bright-colored fabric, signs, a variety of textures, ramps, and any other materials you have available.

- The changes you make should not create a new safety problem.

STEAM Connection

Science	Use research about vision loss to determine changes that can help.
Technology	Take photos before and after making changes.
Engineering	Use materials to make an area of a home safer.
Art	Use color, lines, and shapes to make home features easier to see.
Math	Measure and estimate materials needed to alter an area visually.

Making Places Safer

Research Vision Loss and Visual Safety Measures

Do research to find out more about vision loss and safety. Answer the items below to help you brainstorm on page 60.

1. What tips do groups like the CDC and the NCOA recommend for helping to prevent falls? How can you use them when you change a room in your home? What ideas did you get from this unit? List or draw the ideas.

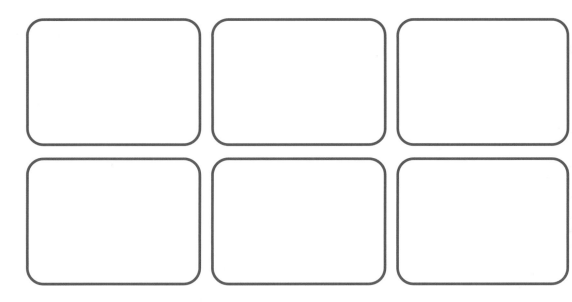

2. Observe three rooms in your home. List a hazard in each room that could possibly cause a fall.

Room 1:

Room 2:

Room 3:

3. List materials you have available to use to change the room.

_____   _____   _____

_____   _____   _____

Skills:
Conduct research;

Make observations;

Use visual information;

Hypothesize;

Answer items based on research and observation

Making Places Safer

Brainstorm Ideas to Redesign the Room

Draw a sketch that shows visual changes you will make to a room in your home to make it safer. Use your answers on page 59 to help you brainstorm ideas.

Making Places Safer

Skill Sharpeners: STEAM • EMC 9336 • © Evan-Moor Corp.

Make a Room Safer with Visual Changes

Skills:
Create changes to a room and take photographs;

Compare and contrast the room before and after your changes;

Formulate opinions;

Reflect on the success of the changes you made;

Practice self-awareness

Take photos of the room before you begin making changes. Then create the visual changes to the room. Last, take photos of all the changes you made.

When you are finished, answer the items below.

1. Look at your before-and-after photos. Show them to other people. Then complete the Venn diagram to compare and contrast how the room was before and after you made changes. Write at least one thing in each part of the Venn diagram.

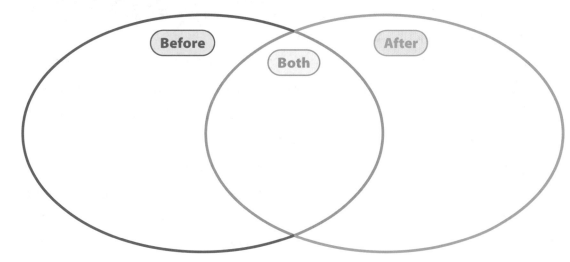

Before   Both   After

2. Do you believe that the room you redesigned is safer now?

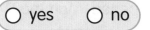 ○ yes   ○ no

3. Make a check mark in the box if you agree with the statement.

☐ Redesigning rooms to make them safer is an issue that is important to me.

☐ Preventing falls caused by vision loss is an issue that I care about.

☐ Learning about how people's abilities may change as they age is interesting.

Making Places Safer

Concepts:
Some people do not have access to transportation and must walk to get things they need;

Some people who do not have transportation must walk through hazardous areas;

Not having access to transportation can make life challenging;

Some people do not have access to shoes

No Transportation

Read the story. Think about the problems in the story.

Tired Feet

It was still dark outside as Abana helped her younger sister get ready to leave for school. The girls had to walk two miles from their small village in Ghana every morning. They had to leave very early to get to school on time. They did not have any shoes to wear, which made the walk even more difficult. Abana often had to carry her little sister because she cried when her feet hurt. Some days the girls were late because the dirt road they walked on was muddy and full of giant puddles. And they also had to watch out for wild baboons along the way, because they could sometimes be aggressive and territorial.

After school Abana and her sister always walked back home. One day when they got home, their mother was nowhere to be found. Abana knew her mother usually walked to the market to collect water or get food in the afternoons, so she told her sister to stay inside the house. Abana went in search of her mother. After walking a mile, Abana found her mother sitting on the side of the road with a large gash in her foot. A container full of water was resting on the ground. Abana cried out, "What happened, Mamma?" Her mother answered that she had cut her foot on a sharp rock. Abana used a scarf to wrap her mother's foot, and they slowly made their way home. Abana carried the water container, and her mother limped along beside her. Abana thought how nice it would be if they only had a bicycle and wouldn't have to walk everywhere.

Skill Sharpeners: STEAM • EMC 9336 • © Evan-Moor Corp.

No Transportation

Skills:
Identify key problems and ideas in a text;

Interpret, analyze, and summarize a problem;

Make connections;

Make inferences;

Rank the importance of problems presented in a story;

Justify an opinion

Answer the items about the story you read.

1. Write three problems in the story in order of importance, from most important to least important.

   Problem 1 _____

   Problem 2 _____

   Problem 3 _____

2. Predict how the outcome of the story would have been different if Abana had *not* gone searching for her mom. Write one difference.

   _____

   _____

3. Read some of the benefits that Abana's family might have if they had a bicycle or a car and could drive instead of walking everywhere. Rank the benefits in order of *1* to *3*, with *1* meaning *most important* and *3* meaning *least important*.

   [ ] It would be easier to carry home items such as containers of water or food.

   [ ] There would be less chance of getting injured from walking barefoot or encountering wildlife.

   [ ] Abana and her sister wouldn't have to leave so early for school.

4. Describe how Abana's life is different from yours due to the difference in transportation options you each have.

   _____

   _____

No Transportation

No Transportation

Bicycles to the Rescue

Many people might take transportation for granted. They can hop on a bus or a train, drive their own car, or get a ride with someone to go to school or work. Many people have access to a set of wheels to use when they run errands. It is not the same for everyone, though. In some places, there are few people who have cars, and in places such as these there is often no form of public transportation. Many people are able to get by without cars, buses, trains, or other forms of transportation, but it can be challenging.

Some people believe that transportation can make life easier in different ways. For one thing, it can help people get from one place to another more quickly. Carrying objects is another thing transportation helps with. When you are walking, you must carry the load on your own body. But when you have a bicycle or another vehicle, you can use the vehicle's mass to help carry the load. Transportation can also help your body. It can be exhausting to walk miles, and it can be hard on your joints and feet.

Villagers in a remote part of India carrying water

In some places, walks can be long and difficult. Some roads are mostly dirt and full of ruts. Many people walk through dangerous terrain with flowing rivers, steep cliffs, and dark forests. In some places, such as India and Alaska, people know which paths can put you at a higher risk of encountering dangerous wildlife. But what if you had to cross through a dangerous area on foot to get things you need, such as food, water, medical attention, or an education?

Skill Sharpeners: STEAM • EMC 9336 • © Evan-Moor Corp.

According to experts on global transportation research, people living in rural areas and people living in poverty are less likely to have access to transportation. People in remote rural areas with no transportation are more at risk of being isolated from other people. And people in remote areas are more likely to travel on foot through hazardous terrain.

A lot of people are trying to help those who have no access to transportation. One company in Seattle, WA, collects donated bikes from all over the world, fixes them up, and ships them to where they are needed. The company also teaches people how to ride bikes. Most of the work is done by volunteers. Volunteers organize community donations of bicycles and parts. There are other organizations that donate bikes, too.

Even though many people around the world are able to survive without transportation, it can make some things easier. That's why there are so many people who donate and accept bicycles.

© Evan-Moor Corp. • EMC 9336 • Skill Sharpeners: STEAM

No Transportation

Make Bicycle Accessories

Riding a bicycle to buy groceries or other items makes some people's lives easier. Many bicycles have special accessories designed to carry things.

Design two accessories for a bicycle that look attractive and also serve a purpose, such as helping to carry things or helping with safety.

Skills:

Convey an idea through visual art;

Explore uses of materials and tools to create works of art or design;

Use observation and investigation in preparation for making a work of art;

Demonstrate creativity;

Follow detailed instructions

What You Need

- bicycle template on page 68
- colored pencils

Things You Might Use

- cardboard
- foil
- mirror
- duct tape
- pipe cleaners
- bubble wrap
- fabric

What You Do

1. Look at the photos of bikes with accessories on page 67.

2. Use the bicycle template on page 68 to design the two accessories you will make. Think about the materials you will use. Be creative and remember to design accessories that have a purpose!

3. Next, make the bicycle accessories.

4. If you'd like, put the accessories on your own bike or give them to someone who has a bike.

No Transportation

basket

bell

bike mirror

water bottle holder

Brainstorm ideas for accessories and draw them on the bicycle.

Saving Time with a Bicycle

Riding a bicycle instead of walking everywhere can save a great deal of time. The extra free time can be used for other things, such as studying or playing sports with family and friends.

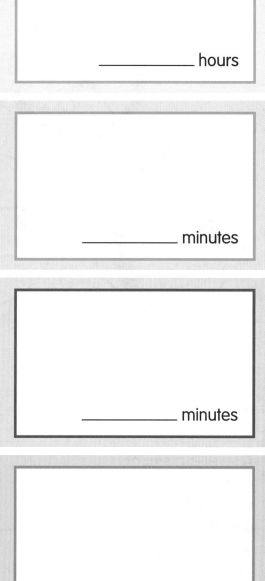

Skills:
Calculate distance and time;
Solve word problems;
Use decimals

Solve the items.

1. Children in a family living outside a rural village must walk 1.5 miles to school each day. They walk at a rate of 3 miles per hour. How long does it take the children to walk to school and back home each day?

   _____ hours

2. The children all got bikes to ride to their school. The children ride their bikes at a rate of 9 miles per hour. How long does it take the children to bike to school and back home each day?

   _____ minutes

3. How much time does biking save the children each day?

   _____ minutes

4. How much time does biking save the children in a five-day school week?

   _____ minutes

No Transportation

Simple Machines and Bikes

People use machines to help make their work easier. There are six basic simple machines: lever, wheel and axle, pulley, inclined plane, wedge, and screw. There are three simple machines in a bicycle. Can you identify them?

Match each simple machine description to the correct bicycle part.

No Transportation

Lever	Pulley	Wheel and Axle
A lever is a straight object that pivots on a hinge point called a fulcrum. You use a lever to help move objects.	A pulley uses one or more wheels with grooves. A chain fits into the grooves and pulls to help move a load or change the direction of the force.	The wheel and axle uses a wheel with a long narrow part attached in the middle to help create movement and move objects.

Skill Sharpeners: STEAM • EMC 9336 • © Evan-Moor Corp.

Bicycle Mechanics

Bicycle mechanics are people who repair or maintain bicycles to keep them working properly. A bicycle mechanic needs to be able to do problem solving. When the mechanic works on a bike that needs repair, he or she studies the bike carefully. Then the mechanic diagnoses the problem, similarly to how a doctor diagnoses a patient. Bicycle mechanics know about simple machines and understand what bikes need to work properly. Volunteers at some of the organizations that donate bikes try to teach people around the world how to repair bikes on their own. The people who receive the donated bikes may also learn some mechanics skills!

Skills:
Learn about the career of a bicycle mechanic;
Make inferences

1. Explain why volunteers would want to teach people in a remote village who are receiving bikes how to repair them on their own.

   _____

   _____

   _____

2. How do bicycle mechanics help keep people safe?

   _____

   _____

3. The text above compares bicycle mechanics and doctors. Write one other similarity between doctors' and bicycle mechanics' work.

   _____

   _____

No Transportation

Skills:
Problem solving;
Creative skills;
Solving problem-based, authentic tasks;
Multiple methods;
Multiple content areas;
Connected ideas;
Technology integration

Problem to Solve

You work for an organization that fixes up old bikes and donates them to different countries. You will create an instructional manual on how to revamp old bikes so they look almost brand new.

Task

Read and answer the items on page 73 to research bikes and instructional manuals. Then, on page 74, brainstorm ideas to design the bike and the manual. Next, revamp a real bike if possible and create your manual. Last, answer the items on page 75.

Rules

- The instructional manual can be digital or hard copy.
- The manual can include any steps you want, including repairing, painting, cleaning, polishing, decorating, or accessorizing.
- The manual must include pictures or photos and should be visually interesting, colorful, and fun to read.

STEAM Connection

Science	Develop a procedure for revamping a bike.
Technology	Create a digital or hard copy, step-by-step manual.
Engineering	Consider repairs and the parts of a bike when revamping it.
Art	Create a manual; revamp a bike or describe how you would revamp it.

No Transportation

Research Bikes and Instruction Manuals

Skills:

Conduct research;

Make observations;

Use visual information;

Hypothesize;

Answer items based on research and observation

Research bicycle designs and ideas for revamping a bicycle.

1. Look at photos of different kinds of bikes. Sketch and label features that you like and might want to include a step for in your manual.

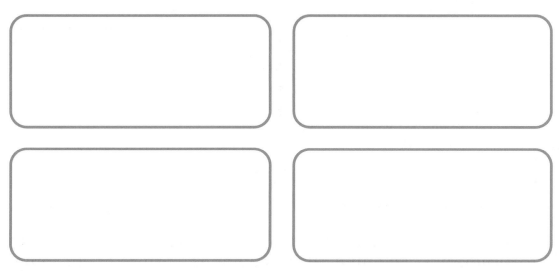

2. Look at other instructional manuals. Write three things you see that you want to include in your own manual.

3. List materials and tools you have available to revamp a bike, if you plan to actually work on a bike. Or, if you do not plan to change a real bike, list materials that you think would be useful for the steps you want to include in your manual.

_____   _____   _____

_____   _____   _____

No Transportation

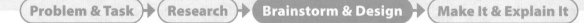

Design the Bike and Manual

Sketch a bike with all of the designs and accessories you want to add. Include colors. List the changes you want to make to the bike, whether you are really working on a bike or not.

Create an outline for your manual. Write each step that you want to include in the manual, such as painting the bike or attaching a basket to the bike. Keep the steps simple. The manual should just include the general changes you want to make to the bike.

No Transportation

Create the Instructional Manual

If you have a bike that you want to revamp and take photos of, make your changes to it before you create your manual. Take photos of the bike, and include them in the manual. If you do not want to revamp a real bike, start creating the manual. Make the manual colorful and interesting to read.

When you are finished making the manual, answer the items below.

1. Think about two of the steps you wrote to revamp the bike. Then write the benefit of each step.

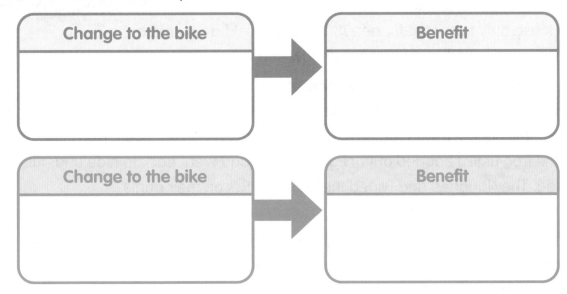

Change to the bike		Benefit
	→	

Change to the bike		Benefit
	→	

2. Do you feel that a lack of transportation is an important global issue? Explain why or why not.

_____

_____

_____

3. Draw an **X** in the box if you agree with the statement.

☐ The manual I created is visually interesting.

☐ The manual would really help someone revamp a bike.

No Transportation

Concepts:

Many people do not wash their hands as often as recommended to prevent the spread of germs;

Sometimes people within a single family spread germs to each other and get sick;

Washing our hands helps us stay healthy and keeps our family and friends healthy;

It is recommended for people to wash their hands before they eat or serve food to others

Read the story. Think about the problems in the story.

Illness in the Family

Joseph and his cousin Paul were playing outside. Joseph's little sister, Sara, was really sick, and relatives had started stopping by the house out of concern for her. At first Sara just had a cough, like Joseph had a week ago, but now she was having trouble breathing.

Joseph and Paul were keeping busy, looking for interesting rocks by a little stream near the house. Joseph spotted a frog under a log and captured it in his hands. It was really muddy and slimy. The boys took turns holding the frog until it hopped out of Paul's hands and went back to hide under its log. They laughed and wiped their dirty hands on their pants.

The boys were hungry, so they went to ask Joseph's mom if they could have something to eat. Since the house was crowded with relatives, Joseph's mom gave the boys a little money and told them they could walk to the nearby plaza and buy some lunch. As the cousins got close to the plaza, the smell of food was wonderful. Joseph and Paul lined up at the pizza place and bought two slices. While they were waiting for their food, Joseph watched one of the workers who was sweeping and picking up garbage from the floor with her bare hands. After the worker finished, she went behind the counter and started serving food to customers. The boys got their pizza slices and ate them as they walked back to Joseph's house, stopping occasionally to pick up interesting rocks along the way.

Skill Sharpeners: STEAM • EMC 9336 • © Evan-Moor Corp.

Handwashing

Illness and Cleanliness

Answer the items about the story you read.

Skills:

Identify key problems and ideas in a text;

Interpret, analyze, and summarize a problem;

Make connections;

Make inferences;

Formulate opinions

1. Write one thing that happened in the story that could possibly cause a problem. Explain why it could lead to a problem.

   _____

   _____

   _____

2. How do you think Joseph's sister might have gotten sick? Write your inference below.

   _____

   _____

   _____

3. Read each statement. Draw an **X** in the box if you agree with it.

   ☐ The employee at the restaurant was picking up garbage from the floor with her hands. Then she started serving food. The employee should have washed her hands before serving food.

   ☐ The cousins should have washed their hands before eating because they touched a muddy frog and rocks.

   ☐ If the boys don't wash their hands when they get home, they could risk making their relatives sick.

4. Choose one of the statements above and write an explanation to justify why you agreed or disagreed with the statement.

   _____

   _____

Handwashing

The Purpose of Handwashing

Did you know that there is a Global Handwashing Day? Every year on October 15th, countries around the world share information about handwashing and how it can help people be healthy. Although medical experts agree that handwashing can help reduce the spread of germs, there are many people around the world who do not wash their hands regularly. One of the best chances of changing this is by teaching people how important handwashing is.

According to the Centers for Disease Control and Prevention, or the CDC, handwashing can help people avoid getting sick and prevent spreading germs to others. The CDC bases this information on many studies on diseases. Everything we touch has microbes, or small living things, such as bacteria. Many microbes do not harm us, but some can cause serious illness. Think about everything you touch in an average day. The refrigerator, television remote, electronic devices, handles on grocery carts, light switches, and doorknobs—they all have microbes. Even people's bodies have microbes. Every single time our hands touch something, tiny microbes transfer to us and from us.

Handwashing

Skill Sharpeners: STEAM • EMC 9336 • © Evan-Moor Corp.

Doctors recommend ways to make handwashing as effective as possible. Effective handwashing requires you to scrub your hands with soap and clean water for at least 20 seconds to wash away the germs. It is recommended to scrub all parts of your hand, including under the fingernails. The CDC emphasizes how important it is to wash your hands properly.

Even though experts have shared how to do handwashing properly, millions of people die each year from illnesses that could have been prevented by effective handwashing. Studies show that children who wash their hands regularly and properly get sick less than children who do not. Some people do not wash their hands regularly because they don't have access to soap and clean water. Other people may not wash their hands because they don't understand how it can help prevent illness.

In addition to sharing how to wash our hands effectively, the CDC also recommends handwashing at these times:

Wash your hands BEFORE	Wash your hands AFTER
preparing food	caring for someone who is sick
eating	using the restroom
treating a cut or wound	touching garbage, changing a diaper, or handling animals

Handwashing is not the only thing we can do to stay healthy, but it is one thing that all medical experts agree can make a difference. This may be the reason so many countries try to educate people about it.

© Evan-Moor Corp. • EMC 9336 • Skill Sharpeners: STEAM

Concepts:
The CDC claims that many diseases are preventable with effective handwashing;

Washing our hands for at least 20 seconds with soap and clean water is recommended;

There are various reasons why people do not wash their hands effectively

Handwashing

Skills:
Convey an idea through visual art;

Explore uses of materials and tools to create works of art or design;

Use observation and investigation in preparation for making a work of art;

Demonstrate creativity;

Follow detailed instructions

Handwashing Reminder Bib

Babies and toddlers often need help washing their hands, and they depend on other people to feed them. This is why it is important for parents and other people who care for children to carefully wash their own hands before preparing food for babies and toddlers.

Design and create a bib that reminds parents, babysitters, and other people who care for children how important it is to wash their hands before serving food.

Things you might choose to use:

- material for the bib such as fabric, plastic, cardboard, or paper

- materials to decorate the bib such as paint, markers, sparkles, glue, tissue paper, foil, uncooked pasta, pipe cleaners, cotton balls, etc.

- pencil

- scissors

- bib template on page 81

What You Do

1. Sketch your ideas on the bib template on page 81. Be sure to include some type of message to remind people to wash their hands.

2. Cut out the template and use it to trace the shape onto the material you will use to make the bib.

3. Decorate the bib using materials you have available. Be sure to include the reminder on the bib. Be creative!

Handwashing

Sketch your design ideas on the bib.

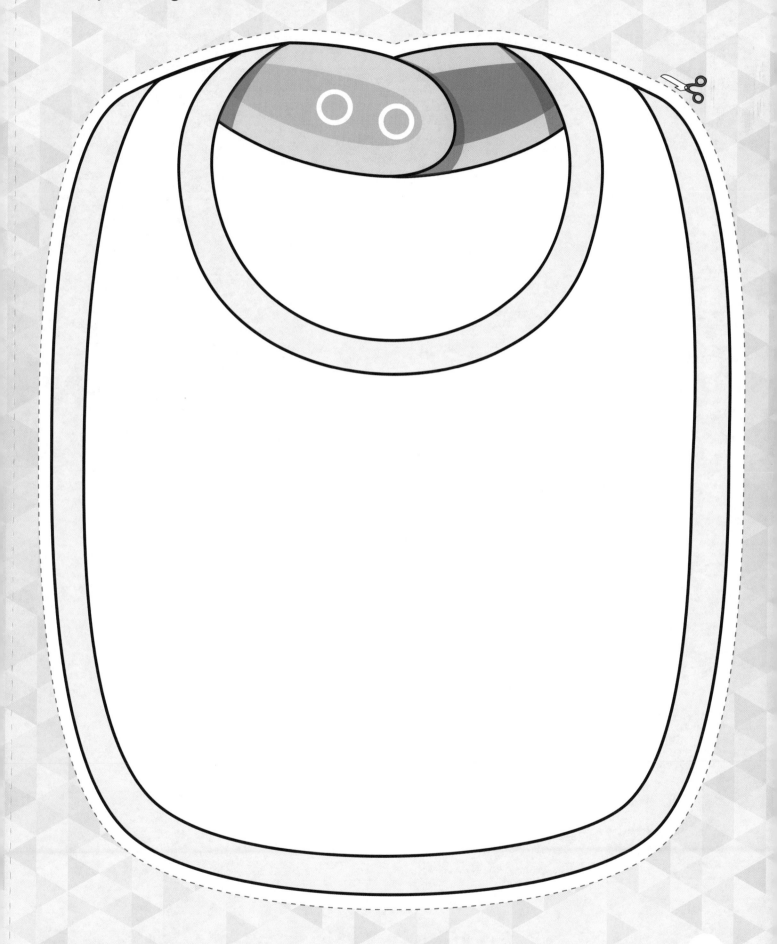

Reducing the Numbers

Skills:
Calculate percentages;
Interpret data in a bar graph;
Use mathematical reasoning

Bacteria are microbes that are found everywhere on Earth. Some bacteria make people and animals sick.

Scientists counted the number of bacteria on the tip of a person's index finger at different times. Study the bar graph and answer the items.

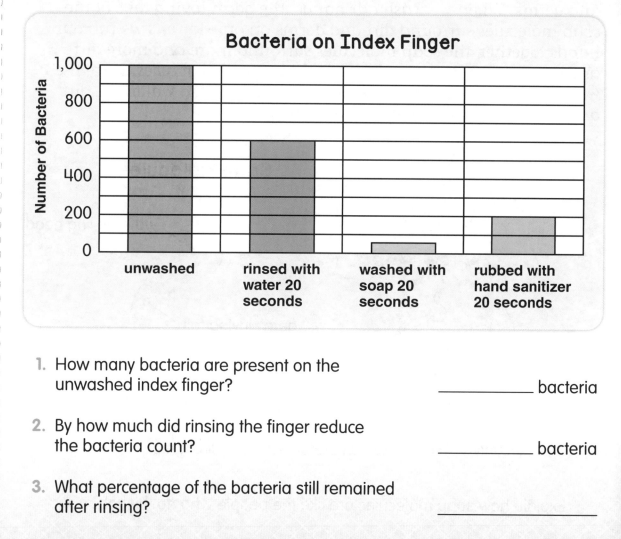

Bacteria on Index Finger

1. How many bacteria are present on the unwashed index finger? _____ bacteria

2. By how much did rinsing the finger reduce the bacteria count? _____ bacteria

3. What percentage of the bacteria still remained after rinsing? _____

4. How many bacteria are on the index finger after using hand sanitizer only? _____ bacteria

5. Which method is best for removing bacteria and why?

_____

_____

Handwashing

The Science of Soap

Research shows that effective handwashing can help stop the spread of disease. What makes soap so effective at getting rid of germs?

Skills:

Learn about soap molecules;

Read a diagram;

Draw upon an analogy to show understanding of how soap bubbles work;

Think critically and creatively;

Compare;

Form a hypothesis

Soap is a chemical made up of many tiny soap molecules. Each tiny molecule has a head that loves water and a tail that loves dirt and germs. When we wash our hands, the germ-loving tails of the soap molecules surround dirt and germs on our skin. As we rub our hands together, the soap molecules surround more and more dirt and germs to create lots of "germ bubbles" called *micelles*. Since the water-loving heads of the molecules are attracted to water, the dirt and germs get washed away in the water.

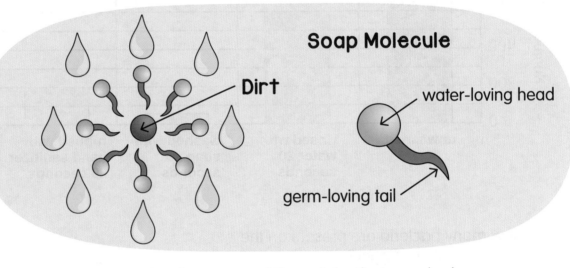

1. Compare soap molecules to one of these jobs that people do:

   security   exterminator   firefighter

   Explain how soap molecules are like the people who do this job.

   _____

   _____

2. What do you think would happen to the germs if you rubbed soap on your hands but you had no water?

   _____

Skill Sharpeners: STEAM • EMC 9336 • © Evan-Moor Corp.

Handwashing

Epidemiologists

Skills:
Learn about epidemiologists;

Use visual information to match pictures to descriptions of important components in epidemiology

The study of how diseases affect people is called *epidemiology*. An epidemiologist is a person who studies diseases and how they spread from person to person. Epidemiologists also study how people can get sick from being exposed to something in the environment, such as polluted air or pesticides. They study how behaviors such as handwashing slow the spread of disease.

The photos show things related to epidemiology. Draw a line to match each photo to its description.

Data:
Epidemiologists collect information and organize it into charts and graphs to analyze the spread of diseases.

Social Science:
Epidemiologists study how groups of people behave to understand how diseases spread.

Technology:
Epidemiologists use computers to store and organize data.

Biology:
Epidemiologists observe germs so they can identify them and learn about them.

Handwashing

Skills:
Problem solving;

Creative skills;

Solving problem-based, authentic tasks;

Multiple methods;

Multiple content areas;

Connected ideas;

Technology integration

Problem to Solve

You work for a volunteer organization that teaches young children how to wash their hands to help prevent the spread of germs and illness. You must create a game that helps children have fun while washing their hands effectively for at least 20 seconds and record someone playing the game.

Task

Read and answer the items on page 87 to research games. Then, on page 88, sketch a picture that shows what your game will look like and write the rules. Next, create the game and record someone playing it. Last, answer the items on page 89.

Rules

- The game must involve objects or materials that can be used with water, such as sponges, cups, buckets, a kiddie pool, lemons, bubbles and bubble wands, bath-time crayons or finger paints, etc.

- The game must involve soap and clean water.

- The recording can show yourself or someone else playing the game.

STEAM Connection

Science	Practice effective handwashing.
Technology	Use a device to record a video.
Engineering	Construct or use materials to make a game.
Art	Create an original game.
Math	Time handwashing for at least 20 seconds.

Handwashing

Research Games with Water

Skills:
Conduct research;
Make observations;
Use visual information;
Hypothesize;
Answer items based on research and observation

Do research to find out more about games with water. Answer the items below to help you design the game and write rules for it.

1. Look at photos of people playing games that involve water. Draw three things you see that you might be interested in including in your game.

2. Fill in the circle next to any items you have available that you want to use.

○ cup   ○ kiddie pool   ○ lemons   ○ bubbles

○ toys   ○ washcloth   ○ bucket   ○ ice cubes

○ apples   ○ soapy sponge   ○ music

○ bath-time crayons or finger paints   ○ sing-along or poem

3. Why do you think that many games designed for young children have sing-alongs?

_____

_____

4. Write answers to each of the following:

The minimum number of people required to play your game: _____

The name of the game: _____

Handwashing

Designing a Game for Young Children

Use your answers to the items on page 87 to help you design the game. Sketch what you envision for the game play below, including the materials needed. Then write the rules.

Write rules for the game you are designing.

_____

_____

_____

_____

_____

_____

_____

Handwashing

Make the Game and Play It!

Skills:

Create an original game to teach handwashing to young children;

Evaluate how fun the game is;

Analyze the decision-making process;

Practice self-awareness

Use your design and rules on page 88 to create the game. Then record a video of someone playing it.

When you are finished recording the video, watch it. Then answer the items below.

1. Explain how you made decisions about the game.

   _____

   _____

   _____

2. Circle *fun* or *not fun* to tell what you thought of the game when you watched the video. Then write three reasons to justify your opinion.

   Fun or Not Fun

   Reason 1: _____

   _____

   Reason 2: _____

   _____

   Reason 3: _____

   _____

3. Is handwashing properly important in your opinion? ○ yes   ○ no

4. Do you think that using a game is a good way to teach something to young children? ○ yes   ○ no

Handwashing

Read the story. Think about the problems in the story.

Kylie's Day

"Divide yourself into four teams!" said the P.E. teacher. Kylie wished the teacher had chosen the teams himself because she felt awkward waiting to be picked. Out of the corner of her eye, she noticed Mary and Adair pointing at her and giggling. Kylie felt her face get red as she heard someone say, "Fine, I guess Kylie's on our team then," followed by a groan.

Later, Kylie still felt lousy from what happened in P.E. "Today you'll work on your projects," Ms. Chatterjee announced in Science. "Find your partners and get to work." Kylie made her way to Mary, her partner, who rolled her eyes as Kylie sat down. Kylie ignored that, though, and suggested making a video for their project.

"No, we're making a poster," Mary retorted. She didn't listen to any of Kylie's other ideas either. Kylie was glad when the class was over.

That night, Kylie's friend Joaquin forwarded a post from Mary: "Kylie eats like a rabbit and looks like one, too." In tears, Kylie called Joaquin.

The next morning, Kylie stopped Mary in the hallway. "I saw what you posted online! A friend showed it to me."

"You have a friend? Shocking!" Mary shot back.

Without even thinking about it, Kylie swung her backpack at Mary. Just then, Mr. Levine, the school counselor, appeared. "Kylie and Mary, please come to my office now," he said sternly.

After listening to both girls, he said, "We're going to talk this through together so I can help you work this out yourselves." Kylie was glad that she'd get a chance to really say how she was feeling in a safe environment.

Skill Sharpeners: STEAM • EMC 9336 • © Evan-Moor Corp.

Bullying

Kylie's Problems

Answer the items about the story you read.

1. Each sentence states a problem in the story. Write numbers to rank the problems from *1* to *3*, with *1* being the *most difficult* or serious problem in your opinion and *3* being the *least difficult* or serious problem.

   ☐ The way other people treat Kylie ruins her day and makes her feel lousy.

   ☐ Kylie does not have a place or a way that feels safe for her to address issues with Mary.

   ☐ Kylie's ideas for her science project are not being considered.

2. Do you think Joaquin's actions in the story were helpful or harmful? Justify your opinion.

   _____

   _____

3. How could the outcome of the story have been different if Mr. Levine had *not* gotten involved? Describe one idea.

   _____

   _____

4. Write one thing Kylie could have done differently in the story.

   _____

   _____

5. Who do you relate to most in the story: Mary, Joaquin, or Kylie? Why?

   _____

   _____

© Evan-Moor Corp. • EMC 9336 • Skill Sharpeners: STEAM

Bullying and Social and Emotional Learning

Have you ever had a bad day or felt unhappy because of how someone treated you? Maybe you've had a day when you felt like you could have been nicer to someone and you felt badly about how you treated that person. Many people have had days like these. The fact is, most of us probably agree that every person deserves to be treated with kindness and respect, but it is hard to be perfect all the time and always do the right thing. We all make mistakes from time to time. When we talk about bullying, though, we are talking about a situation in which someone is regularly being mistreated by another person or a group of people. Bullying is something that happens in different kinds of environments, and it can happen in different ways.

Bullying is recognized by the U.S. government as something that is occurring in schools, although schools are not the only place where bullying can take place. According to the Centers for Disease Control, or the CDC, bullying is defined as "unwanted aggressive behavior." The CDC and the Department of Education describe bullying as a situation in which aggressive behaviors are repeated over and over again. Aggressive behaviors may include spreading rumors, name-calling, or causing physical harm. There are many other ways that bullying can happen.

Cyberbullying is one kind of bullying in which electronic communication or social media is used to bully someone. Bullying can also include damage to personal property. When bullying is taking place, one person or group is trying to use power to control, threaten, or harm someone else. It can be very painful to experience bullying. About 1 in 4 students in the U.S. say they have been bullied. According to the U.S. government, most bullying happens in middle school.

There are different reasons why bullying can happen. According to the U.S. government, research shows that many people who bully have been bullied themselves. For this reason, experts believe that bullying is a complicated problem. If a person is a victim of bullying while also bullying others at the same time, how can schools and parents address these aggressive behaviors and try to prevent them? Scientists who study the brain believe that children learn some of their behaviors by observing others. People start observing and learning behavior from the time they are babies.

Social and Emotional Learning Skills

empathizing with others   making responsible choices   treating others with respect

Scientists and the U.S. government suggest that we can help prevent bullying by creating more awareness about the problem. It is believed that social and emotional skills can be learned, practiced, and developed. Many schools are including social and emotional learning activities in their curriculum. Experts believe that these kinds of skills can help the people who are bullying, as well as the people who are experiencing bullying.

Concepts:
Cyberbullying is when a person is bullied using social media or another digital communication program;
Bullying is recognized by the U.S. government;
Social and emotional learning skills can help students resolve conflicts;
Many people who do bullying were also bullied

Bullying

Skills:
Convey an idea through visual art;

Explore uses of materials and tools to create works of art or design;

Use observation and investigation in preparation for making a work of art;

Demonstrate creativity;

Follow detailed instructions

The Sharing-and-Caring Book

People find themselves in different kinds of situations, and we all react to different scenarios in different ways. How one person feels may not be the same as how another person feels in a similar situation. Different people may react to bullying in many different ways.

You will make a sharing-and-caring book. Write about ways you have been treated or ways you have seen others treated, and express how you felt or what you did when the experience happened.

What You Need

- 2 sheets of blank paper
- stapler
- pencil or pen
- scissors
- tape or glue
- crayons, markers, or colored pencils

What You Do

1. Fold two sheets of paper in half. Staple them along the fold to make a book.

2. Read the scenarios on page 95. These scenarios are examples of how some people have been treated. Think about the ways you have been treated or have seen others be treated. You can think of experiences that made you feel good or bad.

3. On page 96, plan the layout of your book. In the book, write three paragraphs about three separate situations that made you feel a certain way. Next to each paragraph, draw a picture that shows the emotions you felt or how you reacted. It is okay if one of the situations you write about is the same as or similar to one of the scenarios on page 95.

4. Create your book. Make it colorful. Then show it to someone you care about.

Bullying

94

Read the scenarios below to help you create your book.

In the library, you saw a boy drop his calculator, but he didn't notice. Then you saw a friend of yours pick up the calculator and hand it to the boy.

In the school hallway, you saw someone criticizing another student about how he or she was dressed.

You saw a mean comment about one of your friends on social media. The comment had a lot of likes from other people you know.

You and everyone in your class except for one person got an invitation to a classmate's birthday party.

When you arrived at school, you saw a student locker with insults painted all over it.

You walked toward a table in the lunchroom, and the students already there spread out to the ends of the bench to make it look as if there was no more room.

In class you couldn't find your pencil anywhere, and you needed to take notes. A classmate noticed and lent you a pencil.

Bullying

Use the organizer below to plan the layout of your book. Plan the cover and where you will place the words and drawings.

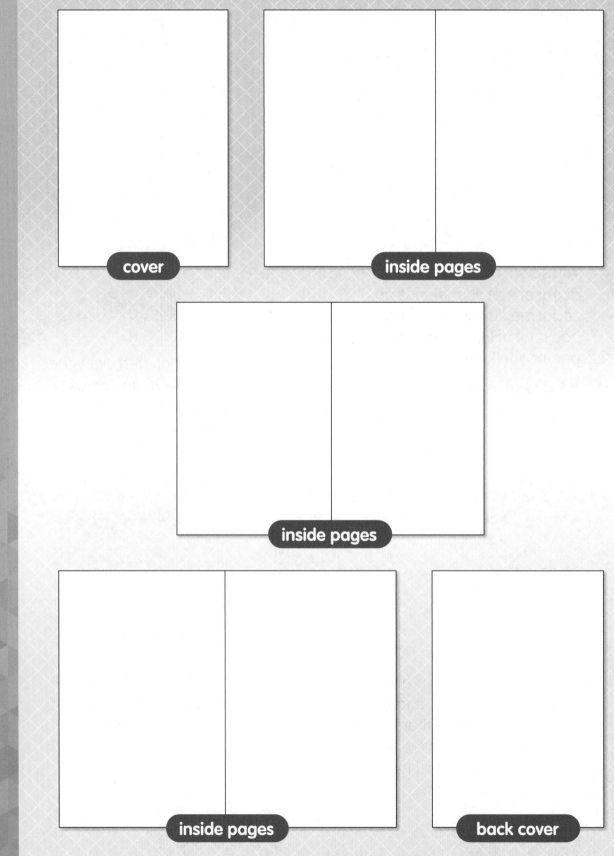

cover

inside pages

inside pages

inside pages

back cover

Skill Sharpeners: STEAM • EMC 9336 • © Evan-Moor Corp.

Using Social Media

Skills:
Understand how social media works;

Consider how social media can be used to practice social and emotional learning

Practice creative thinking

Social media is any form of electronic messaging or communication system. There are many different kinds of social media platforms. Experts in social and emotional learning believe that social media can influence people's moods and happiness.

Read about the social media platforms. Use the descriptions to think about how you could use each platform to brighten someone's day and try to make it better. Write one way you could do this for each platform, and be specific.

Platform	How to use it to make someone's day better
My Frames lets you share videos with others instantly!	_____ _____ _____ _____
Rai\$eMe! helps you raise donations for a cause and also lets you invite your friends to raise money.	_____ _____ _____ _____
With **PetPlay**, you can post photos and videos of your pet, and pets can "request" connections with other pet friends, with the help of their human family members, of course!	_____ _____ _____ _____

Bullying

Facts and Figures on Bullying

Bullying has been around for centuries. Today, cyberbullying, or bullying on social media, is common. But bullying was happening before digital social media even existed.

Use the data below about bullying in the U.S. to answer the items.

- About 1 in every 4 students is bullied.

- An estimated 70% of students have witnessed bullying.

- Being bullied and observing bullying can help cause health problems, including trouble sleeping and headaches.

- It is believed that when bystanders act within the first 10 seconds, they are able to stop bullying from happening about 57% of the time.

- Only about half of the people who experience cyberbullying know who is bullying them.

- Many people who do the bullying have been victims of bullying.

1. About what percent of students are bullied? _____

2. Out of 2,000 people, about how many have probably witnessed bullying? _____ people

3. In one town, there were 400 incidents of bullying in which bystanders acted to help within the first 10 seconds. About how many of those incidents resulted in the bullying being stopped? _____ incidents

4. The chart shows how many incidents of bullying there were in multiple schools last year. Find the mean, median, and mode of the incidents for all four schools.

School	Incidents
Apple Bay	43
Marina	58
Pinehill	61
Cedar	58

    mean = _____

    median = _____

    mode = _____

Bullying

People Who Work in the Field of SEL

Skills:
Learn about a career related to social and emotional learning;

Practice self-awareness;

Learn about responsible decision making

Social and Emotional Learning (SEL) is a field of study that focuses on healthy and responsible ways to express emotions and deal with different situations. Many SEL experts are teachers. SEL experts can help people of all ages develop skills and also help people dealing with bullying. People who work as SEL professionals are able to practice SEL skills themselves.

You can learn more about what an SEL expert's work is about. Read about self-awareness and responsible decision making below. In the empty circles, write one sentence that tells how you have self-awareness and make responsible decisions.

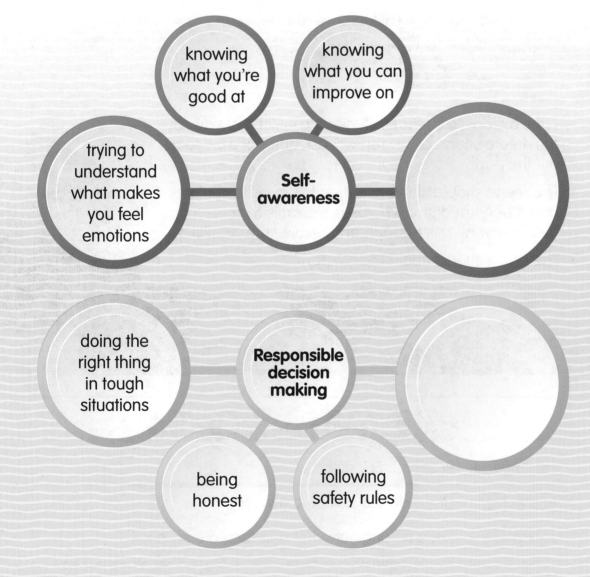

- knowing what you're good at
- knowing what you can improve on
- trying to understand what makes you feel emotions
- **Self-awareness**
- doing the right thing in tough situations
- **Responsible decision making**
- being honest
- following safety rules

Bullying

Problem & Task → Research → Brainstorm & Design → Make It & Explain It

Skills:
Problem solving;
Creative skills;
Solving problem-based, authentic tasks;
Multiple methods;
Multiple content areas;
Connected ideas;
Technology integration

Problem to Solve

Sunny Middle School has been dealing with bullying in recent years. Some students at this school are being trained to become peer mediators. Peer mediators learn SEL skills and try to help their classmates resolve disagreements by talking through problems. You will create a training video of a scene showing how a conflict can be resolved using SEL skills. Write a short script to perform and ask friends or family members to act a role in your video. Then record them as they act it out.

Task

Read and answer the items on page 101 to research some SEL skills and ideas for resolving conflicts. Then, on page 102, draw the scene and write an outline for your script. Next, write the complete script and record the video. Last, answer the items on page 103.

Rules

- Write a story script that includes a conflict that you can turn into a short scene. You will ask other people to act out the parts.

- The scene should show two people having a conflict and a peer mediator who uses SEL skills to calmly help everyone talk through and resolve the conflict.

- The scene should show three actors.

STEAM Connection

Science	Research SEL skills.
Technology	Use a device to record a video.
Art	Write an original script and record a scene.

Bullying

Research SEL Skills for Peer Mediation

Skills:
Conduct research;
Make observations;
Use visual information;
Hypothesize;
Answer items based on research and observation

Do research to find out more about how to resolve conflicts.

1. Watch SEL videos or read SEL tips and strategies. Write four tips for yourself, such as phrases to use, for your script and video.

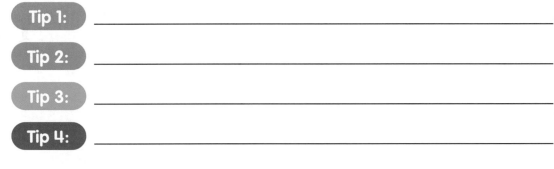

   Tip 1: _____

   Tip 2: _____

   Tip 3: _____

   Tip 4: _____

2. What device will you use to record the video? _____

3. Brainstorm ideas for real conflicts students may have. Write three ideas that you could use for your script and video.

4. Think about a time when you had a conflict with someone else or when you witnessed others having a conflict. Write one thing you experienced or witnessed that you think worked well to help resolve the conflict. Write another thing that you think did not work well.

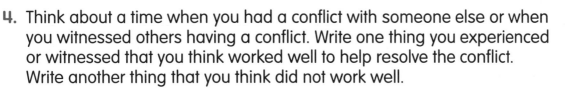

   Well   Not Well

   _____   _____

Skills:

Use concepts to solve a non-routine problem;

Apply concepts;

Write a script outline and plan a training video;

Create a solution to a problem;

Explain a design

Outline Your Script

Draw a picture of the scene showing where each person will be in the scene. Then use your answers from page 101 to help you write your script outline.

Script outline:

_____

_____

_____

_____

_____

_____

_____

_____

Bullying

Skill Sharpeners: STEAM • EMC 9336 • © Evan-Moor Corp.

Record the Training Video Scene

Skills:
Record a training video;

Convey the purpose of the presentation;

Rate the video;

Consider other ways to teach SEL skills;

Reflect on the difficulty of the project

Write the complete script for your video. Rehearse the scene with the actors before you record it. Then record the video and watch it.

After you have recorded the video, answer the items below.

1. Was it more difficult to come up with a story and script for the video or to record the video itself? Explain why.

    _____

    _____

    _____

2. On a scale of *1* to *10*, how realistic was the conflict and scene you created for the video? Write a number with *1* being *unrealistic* and *10* being *very realistic*. _____

    Explain why you answered this way.

    _____

    _____

3. Other than a training video, what other types of training methods could you use to teach students SEL skills and ways to resolve conflicts? Write two.

Bullying

Concepts:

It can be challenging when your community loses a recreation space where you used to hang out with your friends;

Areas designed for recreation provide a safe place for kids to spend time;

Skate parks help reduce the number of people skating in streets and parking lots

Read the story. Think about the problems in the story.

Nowhere to Skate

"I can't believe they really did it!" Priya stared through the chain-link fence, her skateboard in hand. A new sign hung from the fence. There had been rumors that the park was going to close because the town didn't have money to repair it.

"This stinks!" Luciana groaned.

Priya thought about all the fun they'd had perfecting tricks and hanging out in the park. She sighed. "Let's skate someplace else."

Ian pointed at some broken bottles near the fence. "Some high school kids probably did this. I hope they don't start breaking bottles all over town 'cause they're bored, now that the park's closed."

Priya and her friends wandered into town, hoping to find a good place to skate. They suddenly remembered that the convenience store had a long ramp to make shopping easier for people who used wheelchairs.

"Check this out!" Luciana flew down the ramp and did a kickflip. Her skateboard shot out from under her feet and almost hit a customer.

"Watch it!" he yelled.

"Sorry," Luciana quietly replied.

A manager came outside and told the group to skate someplace else. Ian did some ollies on the sidewalk. The board lifted off the ground with his feet. But a couple of moms came along with little children, so he stopped.

Priya sighed. "I guess we have nowhere to skate. What now?"

No one had any ideas, so they all went to Priya's house to watch TV.

PARK CLOSED

Skill Sharpeners: STEAM • EMC 9336 • © Evan-Moor Corp.

What Now?

Skills:

Identify key problems and ideas in a text;

Interpret, analyze, and summarize a problem;

Make connections;

Make inferences;

Produce a creative drawing;

Justify an opinion

Answer the items about the story you read.

1. List three problems in the story.

   Problem 1 _____

   Problem 2 _____

   Problem 3 _____

2. How did the skate park benefit people in the town who didn't even skate?

   _____

   _____

3. Draw two pictures of other activities Priya and her friends could have done other than watching TV.

4. List two possible consequences for the town or the characters in the story if the young skaters in the town never find another place to skate.

   Consequence 1 _____

   Consequence 2 _____

Nowhere to Skate

Investing in Skate Parks

How does a town or city determine what things are most important? There are certain things that are common in most communities. For example, most have schools, police and fire departments, hospitals, grocery markets, and businesses where people work. Many towns have places for recreation and entertainment, too, such as movie theaters, community pools, golf courses, and skate parks. Although many different communities have these things, not everyone agrees on what is most important for a town. So how does a town make the tough decisions about what to invest in?

When a town invests in something, it means that the people of the town think it is important, so they are willing to spend the town's money, resources, and time to have it. Towns have a budget and try to spend their money carefully. For example, a town with lots of damaged roads may decide that repairing the roads is the most important thing to spend money on this year. Another town that has roads in good condition may want to use its money for something else, such as building a skate park, creating a festival, or hiring more firefighters. The taxes that people pay to the government are part of a town's budget. Big cities and small towns alike have budgets and must make decisions about what to invest in.

Why would a community want to spend money on recreation? Some people believe that investing in projects that will give young people safe places to hang out and be physically active is an investment in the town's future. Research shows that people who are active are more likely to be happy and healthy.

Skill Sharpeners: STEAM • EMC 9336 • © Evan-Moor Corp.

Some communities have invested in skate parks. One reason for this may be that skateboarding is a popular sport. Another reason may be that the residents in the town or city showed support for the project. There are about 16 million skateboarders in the United States alone. And research shows that skateboarding is an excellent way of getting exercise, which many communities encourage. Skateboarding can help increase heart rate and cardiovascular health. Research shows that skateboarding can be a full-body workout that can help improve one's coordination, balance, and flexibility. Another reason to invest in a skate park is safety. Because skateboarding is so popular, there are a lot of people who will skateboard with or without a park. If there is no park, skaters might go to other public places such as parking lots and streets. This isn't the safest environment for skaters or for other people passing by. Skate parks are designed for skating, with concrete ramps, curbs, and smooth surfaces, and these parks can help prevent skaters from injuring themselves and others.

The United States has at least two thousand public skate parks. Still, many towns are reluctant to build one. One reason may be that skate parks can be expensive. A medium-sized park could cost around $450,000 to build. This is why communities carefully consider investing in one.

Concepts:
Towns have budgets and must make decisions about what to invest in;

Many communities invest in skate parks because skateboarding is a popular activity;

Skateboarding can be a way to exercise

Nowhere to Skate

Skills:

Convey an idea through visual art;

Explore uses of materials and tools to create works of art or design;

Use observation and investigation in preparation for making a work of art;

Demonstrate creativity;

Follow detailed instructions

Skateboard Deck Artwork

Millions of people enjoy skateboarding, and this is why so many towns and cities invest in a skate park. Skate parks can be beautiful and creative. But did you know that many skateboards themselves are creative displays of art? The main part of a skateboard is called the *deck*. That's the part you stand on. The top is covered in grip tape, which helps your feet stay on the board. The bottom is often covered in graphics or artwork.

Design your own 3-D artwork for a model of a skateboard deck. Your design should show something about yourself or your personality.

What You Need

- cardboard
- colored pencils
- glue

Things You Might Use

- cotton balls, pompoms, construction paper, pipe cleaners, foil, paints, markers, glitter

What You Do

1. Look at the images of skateboard decks on page 109 to get ideas for your own design.

2. Sketch your ideas for a colorful skateboard deck on page 110. Your design should say something about who you are or what you like.

3. Cut out a piece of cardboard in the shape of a skateboard deck.

4. Create your colorful artwork. Use materials you have available to decorate your model.

Nowhere to Skate

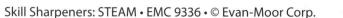

Look at the images of skateboard deck designs.
Brainstorm ideas for your 3-D skateboard deck artwork.

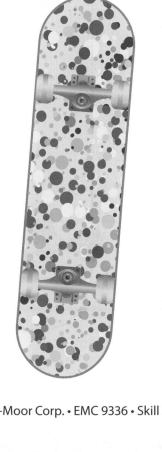

Sketch your ideas below.

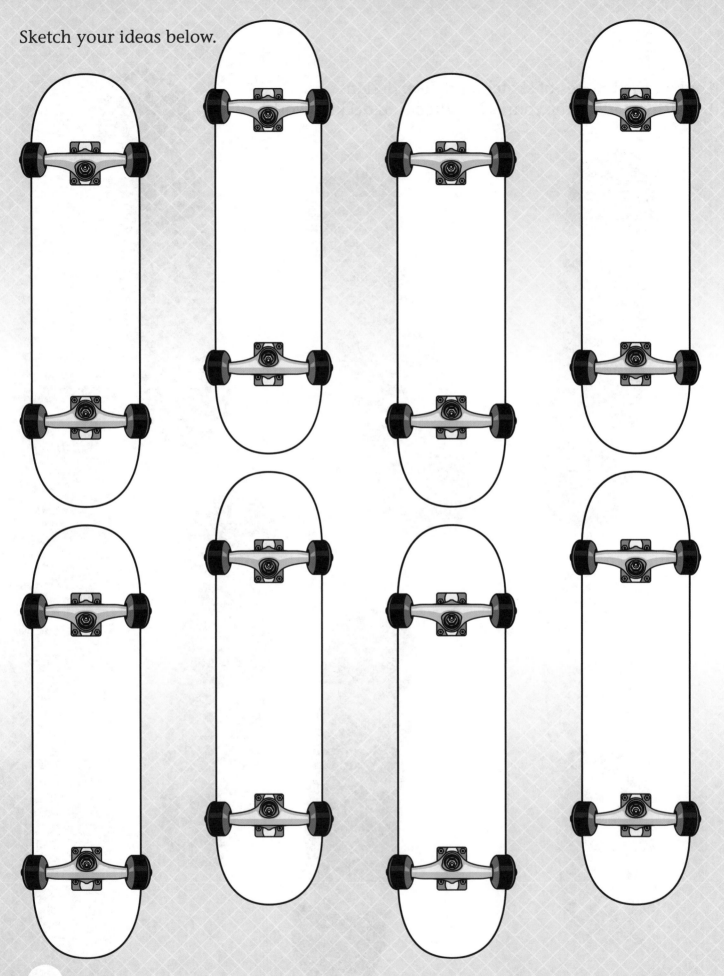

Skateboarding Physics

A skate park is designed especially for skateboarders, who often practice tricks and moves. In skateboard tricks like the ollie, the skateboard leaves the ground with the rider's feet. It looks as if the board is glued to the rider's feet, but, of course, it's not. Gravity keeps people and objects on the ground. It acts on the center of a person or object. By applying force to the back of the skateboard, a rider can make the front pop up. To get the back to lift up, the rider then applies pressure to the front.

Look at the photos. Then answer the items.

1. What do the positions of the skateboards have in common in both of the photos showing ollies? Explain why both boards are like this.

   _____

   _____

   _____

2. Draw a picture of what would happen if a skateboarder tried to do an ollie but could not apply enough force to go against gravity.

Skills:
Use visual information;

Compare and contrast skate park designs and purposes;

Consider purpose and materials to make an inference about cost

Skate Park Construction

There are different kinds of skate parks. Some are outdoors and some are indoors. Some are meant to be permanent and some are set up just temporarily for a competition. Skate park designers build skate parks differently based on the location, their budget, and the park's purpose.

Look at the photos of skate parks being built. Then answer the items.

Park A

Park B

1. Compare and contrast the two skate parks shown. Write one thing in each part of the Venn diagram.

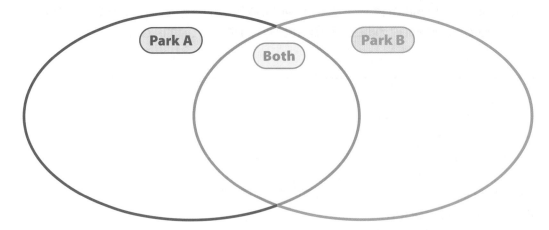

Park A   Both   Park B

2. Which skate park do you think costs less money to build? Which one do you think will stay in good condition for longer? Explain your thinking.

_____

_____

_____

Nowhere to Skate

Skateboard Business

Young skateboarders often dream of being professional skaters. Even if a person does not become a professional skateboarding athlete, he or she can still have a career in that field. Skateboarding magazines, videos, and websites are usually created by people who like to skate themselves. Other jobs in the field include owning a skateboard shop, designing art for skateboards, repairing boards, and designing skate parks.

Skills:
Learn about careers in the field of skateboarding;

Make inferences;

Think creatively;

Make connections;

Practice self-awareness

Answer the items.

1. List six other jobs you can think of that a person might be able to do in the field of skateboarding that is not actually skateboarding.

2. What is your favorite activity? Imagine that you aren't able to do it as a career, but you still want to work in that industry. Describe a job you could do in that industry and why you would like it.

My favorite activity	Job I could do
_____	_____
_____	_____
_____	_____
_____	_____

Nowhere to Skate

Skills:

Problem solving;

Creative skills;

Solving problem-based, authentic tasks;

Multiple methods;

Multiple content areas;

Connected ideas;

Technology integration

Problem to Solve

You work for a company that designs and builds skate parks. You have been hired to make a 3-D model to present to a town committee for the town to build.

Task

Answer the items on page 115 to research skate parks. Then, on page 116, sketch ideas for your skate park model. Next, construct the 3-D skate park model. Last, answer the items on page 117.

Rules

- The skate park model must have at least four features or structures that are typical for skate parks and which skaters can use to do tricks or practice special moves on. These features could include any of the following: a funbox, a handrail, a half-pipe, a bank, a bowl.

- The model must have labels on different features or parts that tell what materials they will be made of when the skate park is built.

- The skate park should have one new, original feature that you came up with.

Nowhere to Skate

STEAM Connection

Science	Consider physics and the purpose of features of a skate park.
Technology	Conduct research; come up with an original design feature for a skate park.
Engineering	Choose realistic skate park materials to label features on the model; construct a 3-D model.
Art	Design and create an original 3-D model.

Research Skate Parks

Skills:

Conduct research;

Make observations;

Use visual information;

Hypothesize;

Answer items based on research and observation

Research skate parks and the purpose of different features of skate parks. Answer the items below to help plan your 3-D model.

1. Watch a skateboarding video to see the moves that skaters do. Then describe an original feature that you will add to your skate park model.

_____

_____

2. Fill in the circle by any materials you have to create the 3-D model.

○ cardboard tubes   ○ cardboard   ○ paper   ○ toothpicks

○ poster board   ○ styrofoam   ○ straws   ○ craft sticks

○ recycled items   ○ aluminum foil   ○ clay

3. Write four features that are common at skate parks. Write what each is usually made of at real parks and how it's used.

Park feature 1:	Park feature 2:	Park feature 3:	Park feature 4:
_____	_____	_____	_____
Materials:	Materials:	Materials:	Materials:
_____	_____	_____	_____
_____	_____	_____	_____
How it's used:	How it's used:	How it's used:	How it's used:
_____	_____	_____	_____
_____	_____	_____	_____
_____	_____	_____	_____

Nowhere to Skate

Sketch Your Model

Make a sketch of what you want your skate park model to look like. Label all the features, including the original one you came up with.

Skills:

Use concepts to solve a non-routine problem;

Apply concepts;

Plan a skate park model;

Create a solution to a problem;

Explain a design

Nowhere to Skate

Skill Sharpeners: STEAM • EMC 9336 • © Evan-Moor Corp.

Build Your Model

Build your model using the design you sketched on page 116. If you'd like, take a photo of your finished model.

After you are finished building the model, answer the items below.

Skills:
Create a model of an original skate park;
Formulate and justify opinions;
Think critically;
Practice self-awareness

1. Read the sentence in the middle, and circle *all* or *not all* to tell how you feel. Then write two reasons for why you feel the way you do.

Reason 1:

I think that all/not all towns should have a skate park.

Reason 2:

2. Do you think that a town owes it to its residents to provide a place for young people to hang out and do recreational activities? Why or why not?

_____

_____

3. What part of your 3-D model are you most proud of and why?

_____

_____

4. Do you think recreation is an issue that is important to the people who make decisions in your community? Justify your opinion.

_____

_____

_____

Nowhere to Skate

Microfinance

Read the story. Think about the problems in the story.

Danso's Farm

The hot, dry air grazed Danso's face as he walked around his family's small farm. The crops his father planted didn't look very healthy. The drought that hit Ghana this year was severe, and the farmers in Bolgatanga were suffering. Danso asked his father if there would be enough to sell at the local market. Danso's father replied, "I am doing my best, but it doesn't look like we will have very much this year because it is so dry."

Danso went back into the house, where his mom was busy weaving a basket. Danso's mom made beautiful baskets whenever she could buy the special grass she needed. She sometimes sold the baskets at the central market. The money she earned helped her family survive. Danso asked his mom, "Do you think you could make lots of baskets and sell them? You could teach me and I could help!"

His mom replied, "I would love to be able to make lots of baskets, but the grass I use comes from the southern part of Ghana and other parts of Africa. I don't have enough money to buy it and have it shipped here."

Danso thought about this. In order for his mom to make money selling baskets, she needed money to buy the materials. Danso remembered one of his friends talking about how his family got a loan of $75 to buy chickens. Now his friend's family sells eggs to make money. Danso wondered if his family could get a loan so his mom could make more baskets.

Earning Money

Skills:

Identify key problems and ideas in a text;

Interpret, analyze, and summarize a problem;

Make connections;

Make inferences;

Justify an opinion

Answer the items about the story you read.

1. Describe how one problem in the story causes another problem.

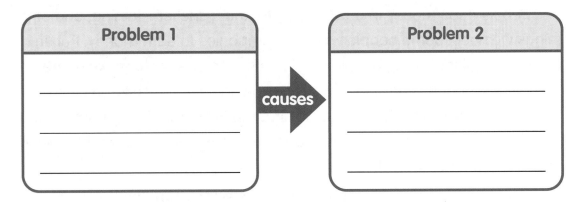

Problem 1		Problem 2
	causes	

2. Explain how a loan could help Danso's family.

_____

_____

_____

3. Complete the sentence to compare how Danso's mother and father make money for the family.

> They both depend on _____
>
> to make money for the family. This makes it challenging to make
>
> money because _____.

4. Are there any problems with the solution that Danso came up with? Explain.

_____

_____

Microfinance

Creating a Path to Earn Money

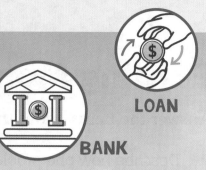

BANK

LOAN

People need money in order to pay for food, shelter, clothing, and other things we need. Some people work for companies to earn money. But, in many parts of the world, people must find their own way to make money. Sometimes, people start a family business, and even the children help out. The problem is that it takes money to start a business in the first place. Some people have an idea for a business and are willing to work hard, but they do not have enough money to start the business.

Banks loan money to people to start a business. When a bank loans money, it expects people to pay back all of the money plus interest. *Interest* is a kind of fee. For example, if a person wants to borrow $10,000 and the bank charges 10% interest, the borrower would have to pay $11,000 in total when he or she pays back the money. That's $10,000 plus ten percent of ten thousand, or $1,000. To get a bank loan, people usually need to show their work history, or show proof that they have been working regularly and making money for years. Most banks also expect people to have collateral. *Collateral* is something you own that is worth money, such as a car or a house.

In some places, it is not easy for a person to get a loan because the person does not have any proof of a work history. Some areas do not have many choices for jobs. There are places in the world that do not have restaurants, gyms, or office buildings. Imagine if you grew up in a small village and there were no towns nearby. What if you had only ever worked on your own family's farm and you never got paid? You probably wouldn't have a work history or collateral.

A young girl works in a tent at her family's market.

Microfinance

Skill Sharpeners: STEAM • EMC 9336 • © Evan-Moor Corp.

Microloan

There are other loan options, though. Microfinancing is when a company loans small amounts of money, called *microloans*, to people. The amounts are often less than $100. People who get microloans do not need a work history or collateral, but they do have to pay back the money, and there is still an interest fee. Many companies that give out microloans set up schedules in which the person pays back the loan in small amounts that are easier to manage.

Many people have benefited from microloans. A lot of people use the money they borrow to buy chickens, cows, or other livestock so that they can sell milk and other products. Some people use the microloans to buy equipment they need, such as wheelbarrows or wood to make fences. If the business is making purses or baskets, materials such as thread or fabric may be bought with the microloan.

Individual people can donate money to families, too. Some websites allow people to make a charitable donation, not a loan, so the money does not need to be paid back. Whether people get money from a loan, a microloan, or a donation, the money can be very helpful for starting a business. For example, a man living in a plastic tent in Colombia borrowed $95 and started up a convenience store in his tent. Within a year, he had enough money to move his family into a house, and he continued to run a successful store. A woman in Pakistan with nine children borrowed $70 to start a jewelry business. The business was so successful that she started a restaurant and catering business and is putting her children through school. Inspiring stories like these may be the reason why so many people think microfinancing is a good idea.

Family members work on their small poultry farm, which they started using a microloan.

Concepts:

Microfinancing is when someone receives a small loan to help with their business;

Starting and running a business requires money;

Many people benefit from microloans;

Microfinancing helps people who may not be able to get a traditional bank loan;

Individuals can donate money online to family businesses

Microfinance

Basket Weaving

There are many different ways to weave baskets and also many different types of baskets to make. Around the world, baskets are used by millions of people for a lot of different purposes. What kind of basket would you make?

Most baskets are made with plant material, but other materials, such as horsehair, can also be used. In this activity, you will create your own basket using paper or fabric.

What You Need

- fabric or construction paper
- ruler
- scissors
- glue

What You Do

1. First, decide what colors you want your basket to be. Will it be all one color, two colors, or multiple colors?

2. After you choose your colors, figure out how many strips of each color of paper or fabric you will need. The bottom of the basket requires 8 strips that are each 1 inch wide and 14 inches long. Cut the paper or fabric into strips using a ruler to measure and make them straight.

3. Arrange half of the strips side by side vertically on your work surface. They should be close together and arranged in the pattern you want, for example, alternating colors.

4. Take one of the other strips, which you did not arrange vertically, and weave it under and over the vertical strips, making sure it is centered so an equal amount sticks out on both sides.

Microfinance

Skill Sharpeners: STEAM • EMC 9336 • © Evan-Moor Corp.

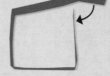

5. Repeat with the remaining strips that are not arranged vertically.

6. Adjust the strips so everything is centered and balanced. Then lift the strip in the top-left corner and glue it to the strip below. Use a small amount of glue. Repeat this on the other three corners.

7. Fold up the strips to form the sides of the basket.

8. Cut four strips that are 18 inches long and 4 inches wide.

9. Mark and fold one of these strips every 4 inches. This will make four sections that are 4 inches long and one section that is 2 inches long.

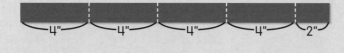

10. Glue the 2-inch section to the first 4-inch section of the strip to form a square.

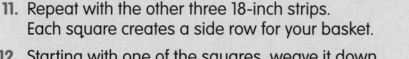

11. Repeat with the other three 18-inch strips. Each square creates a side row for your basket.

12. Starting with one of the squares, weave it down through the strips that are folded up from the bottom on all four sides. Push this square all the way down to make the first row.

13. Repeat with the other three squares.

14. Finish your basket by gluing the top edges of the vertical strips to the top horizontal strip. You will need to do this both inside and outside.

15. Trim the top of the basket so that it is even.

16. Cut a strip that is 18 inches long and 1 inch wide to make a handle. Glue the ends of the handle to the inside of your basket on opposite sides.

Exchange Rates

Countries around the world use different types of money, or currency. When we loan money, it gets converted to whatever currency is used in a particular country. The conversion rate can vary daily.

The bar graph shows the conversions from $1.00 (one U.S. dollar) into the currency for different countries. Use the graph to answer the items.

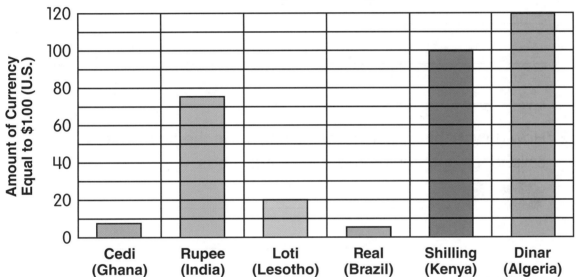

Currency Exchange Rates

Amount of Currency Equal to $1.00 (U.S.)

Cedi (Ghana) · Rupee (India) · Loti (Lesotho) · Real (Brazil) · Shilling (Kenya) · Dinar (Algeria)

1. Approximately how many Kenyan shillings are equal to $1.00 U.S.? _____

2. About how many U.S. dollars would you have to pay if something costs 140 Indian rupees? _____

3. Which country on the graph has currency that is closest in value to the U.S. dollar? _____

   Explain your reasoning.

   _____

   _____

Microfinance

Skills:

Make inferences;

Formulate and justify an opinion;

Consider technology's role in helping people get microloans

Technology and Microfinance

In many places, people who need money do not have access to a bank. However, modern technology enables people in remote areas to access loans.

Thanks to online microfinance sites, people can use their mobile phone to get a microloan.

1. Do you think technology has made it easier for people to donate money and get microloans? Explain your thinking.

_____

_____

_____

2. How do you think people got microloans in the past, before cellphones and the Internet? Write two ideas.

Idea 1: _____

_____

Idea 2: _____

_____

Microfinance

Starting a Business

People start businesses for different reasons. Many children have started their own businesses, too. There are certain things to decide on when starting a business. Read the descriptions and examples below. Then brainstorm ideas for two different businesses you would start if you could.

© Asia Images / Shutterstock.com

Skills:
Learn about starting a business;
Think creatively

Name: What would the name of the business be?

Product or service: What would the business make or do to earn money?

Who: Who would you sell to? You could sell to children, adults, musicians, athletes, or other groups of people. Who would want to pay for your product or service?

Examples of products that a business could make:

bicycle parts   video games   exercise equipment   chairs

Examples of services that a business could provide:

washing cars   repairing skateboards   mowing lawns   cutting hair

Name:

_____

Product or service:

_____

Who:

_____

Name:

_____

Product or service:

_____

Who:

_____

Microfinance

Skills:

Problem solving;

Creative skills;

Solving problem-based, authentic tasks;

Multiple methods;

Multiple content areas;

Connected ideas;

Technology integration

Problem to Solve

Imagine that you work at a microfinancing company. You help families earn more money. Now you are helping a family that has a small plot of land that is 10 feet by 10 feet. They want to start a business but have no money and no idea what to do. You will create a business model to help the family start a business.

Task

Read and answer the items on page 129 to research businesses. Then, on page 130, draw a sketch and write a business model. Next, create a large display of your plan. Last, answer the items on page 131.

Rules

- The business model must be presented on a colorful tri-fold poster board display.

- The business plan must be creative and realistic.

- The business plan must take into account the space the family has.

STEAM Connection

Science	Consider options for a realistic business plan.
Technology	Conduct research.
Engineering	Consider the space available for a business plan.
Art	Create a presentation of a business idea.
Math	Estimate the use of a given amount of space.

Microfinance

Skill Sharpeners: STEAM • EMC 9336 • © Evan-Moor Corp.

Learning About Business

Do research to find out more about businesses. Answer the items below to help you create a business plan on page 130.

Skills:
Conduct research;
Make observations;
Use visual information;
Hypothesize;
Answer items based on research and observation

1. Find photos that show different ways to use a plot of land. Write notes or sketch ideas you get from your research that could be useful for a business.

2. List five things that a successful business needs.

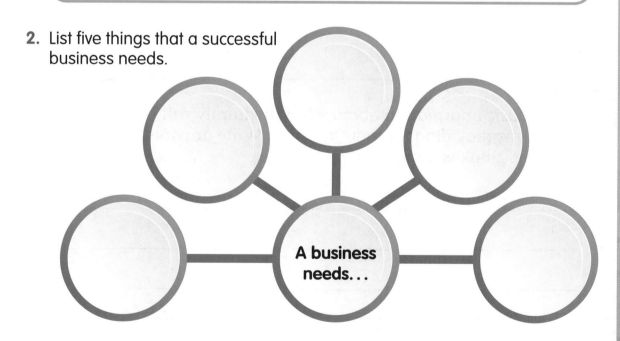

A business needs...

3. What are some businesses a family could do in which the children can help, too? List some ideas.

_____   _____

_____   _____

Microfinance

Sketch and Outline the Business Model

Draw a sketch to show your idea for what the family will be doing for their business. The picture should show how the small plot of land will be used, and it can show the family working. Then outline your business model.

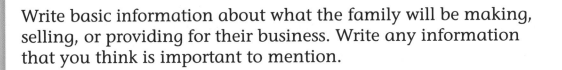

Write basic information about what the family will be making, selling, or providing for their business. Write any information that you think is important to mention.

_____

_____

_____

_____

_____

_____

Microfinance

130

Create a Display

Use the plan you created on page 130 to construct the tri-fold display. It should be colorful and persuasive so that your microfinancing company will want to lend money to the family.

After you finish making the display, answer the items below.

1. Show the display you created to three adults. Ask them if they would lend money to the family based on the display and business model. Record their responses.

Adult 1	Adult 2	Adult 3
○ yes ○ no	○ yes ○ no	○ yes ○ no

2. Do you think that microfinancing is good, bad, or neither good nor bad? Explain your opinion.

_____

_____

_____

3. Other than using a tri-fold display to share a business model, what are other ways that you could present the information? Draw and label three different ways you could do this.

_____   _____   _____

Microfinance

Congratulations!

_____
Name

Science   Technology   Engineering   Art   Math

You went FULL **STEAM** AHEAD
and finished the book!

Cut out the pieces. Put them together to find out what the picture shows.
Then glue them onto construction paper to make a poster.

Puzzle size 22" × 9"

Answer Key

Page 7

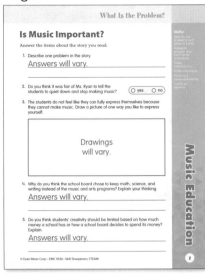

Is Music Important?

Answer the items about the story you read.

1. Describe one problem in the story.
   <u>Answers will vary.</u>

2. Do you think it was fair of Ms. Ryan to tell the students to quiet down and stop making music? ○ yes ○ no

3. The students do not feel like they can fully express themselves because they cannot make music. Draw a picture of one way you like to express yourself.

   Drawings will vary.

4. Why do you think the school board chose to keep math, science, and writing instead of the music and arts programs? Explain your thinking.
   <u>Answers will vary.</u>

5. Do you think students' creativity should be limited based on how much money a school has or how a school board decides to spend its money? Explain.
   <u>Answers will vary.</u>

Music Education

Page 13

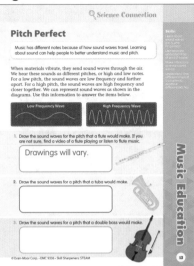

Pitch Perfect

Music has different notes because of how sound waves travel. Learning about sound can help people to better understand music and pitch.

When materials vibrate, they send sound waves through the air. We hear these sounds as different pitches, or high and low notes. For a low pitch, the sound waves are low frequency and farther apart. For a high pitch, the sound waves are high frequency and closer together. We can represent sound waves as shown in the diagrams. Use this information to answer the items below.

Low Frequency Wave   High Frequency Wave

1. Draw the sound waves for the pitch that a flute would make. If you are not sure, find a video of a flute playing or listen to flute music.

   Drawings will vary.

2. Draw the sound waves for a pitch that a tuba would make.

3. Draw the sound waves for a pitch that a double bass would make.

Music Education

Page 14

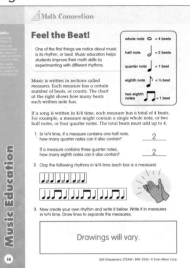

Feel the Beat!

One of the first things we notice about music is its rhythm, or beat. Music education helps students improve their math skills by experimenting with different rhythms.

whole note	= 4 beats
half note	= 2 beats
quarter note	= 1 beat
eighth note	= ½ beat
two eighth notes	= 1 beat

Music is written in sections called measures. Each measure has a certain number of beats, or counts. The chart at the right shows how many beats each written note has.

If a song is written in 4/4 time, each measure has a total of 4 beats. For example, a measure might contain a single whole note, or two half notes, or four quarter notes. The total beats must add up to 4.

1. In 4/4 time, if a measure contains one half note, how many quarter notes can it also contain? <u>2</u>

   If a measure contains three quarter notes, how many eighth notes can it also contain? <u>2</u>

2. Clap the following rhythms in 4/4 time (each box is a measure):

3. Now create your own rhythm and write it below. Write it in measures in 4/4 time. Draw lines to separate the measures.

   Drawings will vary.

Music Education

Page 15

Sound Engineers

Read about the career of sound engineers. Then follow the steps below to practice the skills that sound engineers use.

Sound engineers are people who work to make music sound a certain way. They work in music recording studios, television studios, and in concert halls. A sound engineer's job is to control the sound levels and outputs so that everything sounds balanced to the audience. If working in a recording studio, the sound engineer is also responsible for editing and mixing the soundtrack. Sound engineers need computer and mechanical skills. They also may have music skills.

1. Use a device to make an audio recording. You can use a computer, phone, tablet, or other device. You can record yourself singing or a song, outdoor nature sounds, or something else.

2. Listen to the recording you made. Then use the device to try to edit the audio recording as much as you can. Try to make the recording sound different from its original version.

3. Listen to the new audio recording that you engineered.

Answer the items.

4. Did you have success in changing the original audio recording to make a new sound? Explain your answer.
   <u>Answers will vary.</u>

5. Do you think you would enjoy being a sound engineer? Explain.
   <u>Answers will vary.</u>

Music Education

Page 21

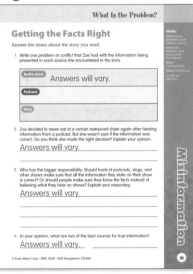

Getting the Facts Right

Answer the items about the story you read.

1. Write one problem or conflict that Zoe had with the information being presented in each source she encountered in the story.

   Radio show | Answers will vary.
   Podcast
   Vlog

2. Zoe decided to never eat at a certain restaurant chain again after hearing information from a podcast. But she wasn't sure if the information was correct. Do you think she made the right decision? Explain your opinion.
   <u>Answers will vary.</u>

3. Who has the bigger responsibility: Should hosts of podcasts, vlogs, and other shows make sure that all the information they hear on their show is correct? Or should people make sure they know the facts instead of believing what they hear on shows? Explain your reasoning.
   <u>Answers will vary.</u>

4. In your opinion, what are two of the best sources for true information?
   <u>Answers will vary.</u>

Misinformation

Page 27

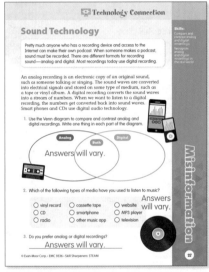

Sound Technology

Pretty much anyone who has a recording device and access to the Internet can make their own podcast. When someone makes a podcast, sound must be recorded. There are different formats for recording sound—analog and digital. Most recordings today use digital recording.

An analog recording is an electronic copy of an original sound, such as someone talking or singing. The sound waves are converted into electrical signals and stored on some type of medium, such as a tape or vinyl album. A digital recording converts the sound waves into a stream of numbers. When we want to listen to a digital recording, the numbers get converted back into sound waves. Smart phones and CDs use digital audio technology.

1. Use the Venn diagram to compare and contrast analog and digital recordings. Write one thing in each part of the diagram.

   Analog | Both | Digital
   Answers will vary.

2. Which of the following types of media have you used to listen to music?
   ○ vinyl record ○ cassette tape ○ website
   ○ CD ○ smartphone ○ MP3 player
   ○ radio ○ other music app ○ television
   Answers will vary.

3. Do you prefer analog or digital recordings?
   <u>Answers will vary.</u>

Misinformation

Page 28

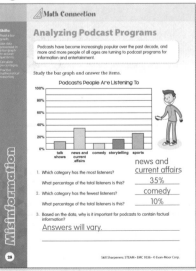

Analyzing Podcast Programs

Podcasts have become increasingly popular over the past decade, and more and more people of all ages are turning to podcast programs for information and entertainment.

Study the bar graph and answer the items.

Podcasts People Are Listening To

talk shows | news and current affairs | comedy | storytelling | sports

1. Which category has the most listeners? <u>news and current affairs</u>
   What percentage of the total listeners is this? <u>35%</u>

2. Which category has the fewest listeners? <u>comedy</u>
   What percentage of the total listeners is this? <u>10%</u>

3. Based on the data, why is it important for podcasts to contain factual information?
   <u>Answers will vary.</u>

Misinformation

Page 29

Podcast Editors

After a podcast is recorded, it usually needs some editing. Editing involves cutting out parts of the recording and changing the parts that are unclear or have mistakes and unwanted noises, such as coughs and sneezes. Sometimes, podcast editors add sound effects or music. A podcast editor has an important role in making sure that the podcast is accurate and doesn't have misinformation. Sometimes, the host or creator of the podcast is the same person who edits it.

1. What is the biggest responsibility of a podcast editor: to make sure that the podcast is entertaining or to make sure there is no misinformation? Explain your opinion.
   <u>Answers will vary.</u>

2. What are some skills that a podcast editor must have? Fill in the circles next to any you think are important. <u>Answers will vary.</u>
   ○ athletic skills ○ creativity ○ attention to detail
   ○ computer skills ○ writing skills ○ technology skills

3. Is podcast editing something you think you would enjoy? Explain why or why not.
   <u>Answers will vary.</u>

Misinformation

Page 35

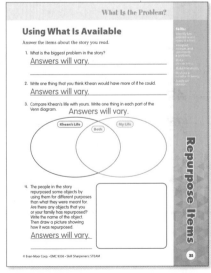

Using What Is Available

Answer the items about the story you read.

1. What is the biggest problem in the story?
   <u>Answers will vary.</u>

2. Write one thing that you think Khean would have more of if he could.
   <u>Answers will vary.</u>

3. Compare Khean's life with yours. Write one thing in each part of the Venn diagram. <u>Answers will vary.</u>

   Khean's Life | Both | My Life

4. The people in the story repurposed some objects by using them for different purposes than what they were meant for. Are there any objects that you or your family has repurposed? Write the name of the object. Then draw a picture showing how it was repurposed.
   <u>Answers will vary.</u>

Repurpose Items

Page 41

Technology Connection

Reusing and Repurposing

People can repurpose items and use them for new things. This can help people save money and avoid being wasteful. We can also make things that are useful out of natural materials. For example, we use cornstalks to make scarecrows, which help scare away pests from crops.

Look at the photos. Draw an **X** beside each one that shows something being repurposed.

In some places, coconuts grow naturally and are plentiful. Coconut shells can be used to make bowls. Think of another way that a coconut shell could be changed or used by people. Write it below.

Answers will vary.

Repurpose Items

Page 42

Engineering Connection

Repurposed Objects

Many things are designed for a specific purpose. But a lot of objects can be repurposed and used for different tasks. Many people are creative with their uses of objects!

Look at the photos. Then answer the items.

1. Which object could be repurposed and used to create a goal area for a soccer game? Explain your thinking.
   Answers will vary.

2. Which object could be repurposed and used as a dish to eat from? Explain your thinking.
   Answers will vary.

Repurpose Items

Page 43

Career Spotlight

Being Resourceful

People often have to be resourceful and creative. People who are resourceful find clever ways to repurpose items. Teachers often repurpose objects in their classrooms to help them teach. Much of the time, people repurpose items in order to meet their needs. Repurposing items can save money and get the most use out of objects. Look at the photos. Read about how some people use the objects shown. Then write two other ideas for how to use each object.

Some people use dental floss to slice foods such as cake or cheese. Eagle Scouts will sometimes use dental floss instead of thread to sew buttons onto clothing.

Idea 1: Answers will vary.
Idea 2: _____

Some people use clothespins in their hair. Teachers use clothespins for art projects. Many people use clothespins for what they were originally designed for—hanging clothes.

Idea 1: Answers will vary.
Idea 2: _____

Repurpose Items

Page 49

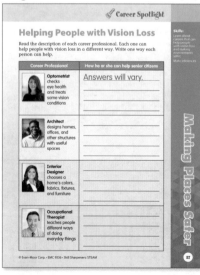

What Is the Problem?

Grandpa's Safety

Answer the items about the story you read.

1. Describe two problems in the story.

Problem 1	Problem 2
Answers will vary.	

2. What do you think caused Marla to need crutches? Explain your thinking.
   Answers will vary.

3. Why do you think there are nurses to help out at Grandpa's new home?
   Answers will vary.

4. Write two suggestions for how the building Raffi's grandpa lives in could be changed to make it safer for people who might not be able to see as well as they used to.

Suggestion 1	Suggestion 2
Answers will vary.	

Making Places Safer

Page 55

Science Connection

Some Vision Loss Conditions

People with different eye conditions may experience different forms of vision loss:
Macular degeneration makes the shape of objects look crooked or covers objects with a dark smudge.
Glaucoma can cause side vision loss or total side vision blindness.
A **cataract** makes everything look cloudy or blurry.

Look at each photo. Write which condition each photo represents, based on the information provided above.

cataract   glaucoma   macular degeneration

Explain how each condition could possibly lead to someone falling.

Macular degeneration: Answers will vary.

Glaucoma: _____

Cataract: _____

Making Places Safer

Page 56

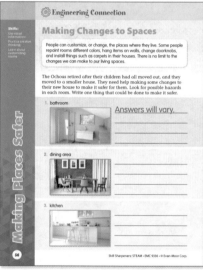

Engineering Connection

Making Changes to Spaces

People can customize, or change, the places where they live. Some people repaint rooms different colors, hang items on walls, change doorknobs, and install things such as carpets in their houses. There is no limit to the changes we can make to our living spaces.

The Ochoas retired after their children had all moved out, and they moved to a smaller house. They need help making some changes to their new house to make it safer for them. Look for possible hazards in each room. Write one thing that could be done to make it safer.

1. bathroom   Answers will vary.

2. dining area

3. kitchen

Making Places Safer

Page 57

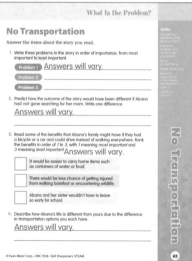

Career Spotlight

Helping People with Vision Loss

Read the description of each career professional. Each one can help people with vision loss in a different way. Write one way each person can help.

Career Professional	How he or she can help senior citizens
Optometrist checks eye health and treats some vision conditions	Answers will vary.
Architect designs homes, offices, and other structures with useful spaces	
Interior Designer chooses a home's colors, fabrics, fixtures, and furniture	
Occupational Therapist teaches people different ways of doing everyday things	

Making Places Safer

Page 63

What Is the Problem?

No Transportation

Answer the items about the story you read.

1. Write three problems in the story in order of importance, from most important to least important.
   Problem 1   Answers will vary.
   Problem 2
   Problem 3

2. Predict how the outcome of the story would have been different if Abana had *not* gone searching for her mom. Write one difference.
   Answers will vary.

3. Read some of the benefits that Abana's family might have if they had a bicycle or a car and could drive instead of walking everywhere. Rank the benefits in order of 1 to 3, with 1 meaning *most important* and 3 meaning *least important*. Answers will vary.
   ☐ It would be easier to carry home items such as containers of water or food.
   ☐ There would be less chance of getting injured from walking barefoot or encountering wildlife.
   ☐ Abana and her sister wouldn't have to leave so early for school.

4. Describe how Abana's life is different from yours due to the difference in transportation options you each have.
   Answers will vary.

No Transportation

Page 69

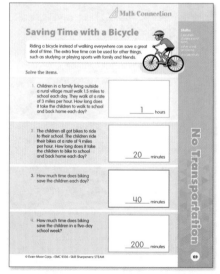

Math Connection

Saving Time with a Bicycle

Riding a bicycle instead of walking everywhere can save a great deal of time. The extra free time can be used for other things, such as studying or playing sports with family and friends.

Solve the items.

1. Children in a family living outside a rural village must walk 1.5 miles to school each day. They walk at a rate of 3 miles per hour. How long does it take the children to walk to school and back home each day?
   1 hours

2. The children all got bikes to ride to their school. The children ride their bikes at a rate of 9 miles per hour. How long does it take the children to bike to school and back home each day?
   20 minutes

3. How much time does biking save the children each day?
   40 minutes

4. How much time does biking save the children in a five-day school week?
   200 minutes

No Transportation

Page 70

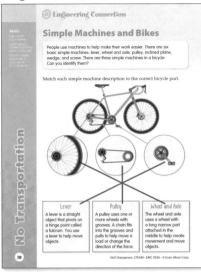

Page 71

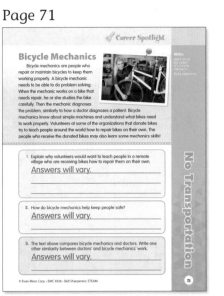

Bicycle Mechanics

1. Explain why volunteers would want to teach people in a remote village who are receiving bikes how to repair them on their own.
   Answers will vary.

2. How do bicycle mechanics help keep people safe?
   Answers will vary.

3. The text above compares bicycle mechanics and doctors. Write one other similarity between doctors' and bicycle mechanics' work.
   Answers will vary.

Page 77

Illness and Cleanliness

Answer the items about the story you read.

1. Write one thing that happened in the story that could possibly cause a problem. Explain why it could lead to a problem.
   Answers will vary.

2. How do you think Joseph's sister might have gotten sick? Write your inference below.
   Answers will vary.

3. Read each statement. Draw an **X** in the box if you agree with it.

   ☐ The employee at the restaurant was picking up garbage from the floor with her hands. Then she started serving food. The employee should have washed her hands before serving food. Answers will vary.

   ☐ The cousins should have washed their hands before eating because they touched a muddy frog and rocks.

   ☐ If the boys don't wash their hands when they get home, they could risk making their relatives sick.

4. Choose one of the statements above and write an explanation to justify why you agreed or disagreed with the statement.
   Answers will vary.

Page 83

Reducing the Numbers

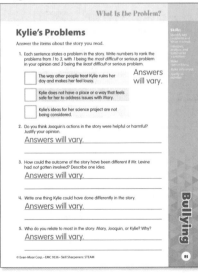

1. How many bacteria are present on the unwashed index finger? **1,000** bacteria
2. By how much did rinsing the finger reduce the bacteria count? **400** bacteria
3. What percentage of the bacteria still remained after rinsing? **60%**
4. How many bacteria are on the index finger after using hand sanitizer only? **200** bacteria
5. Which method is best for removing bacteria and why?
   Answers will vary.

Page 84

The Science of Soap

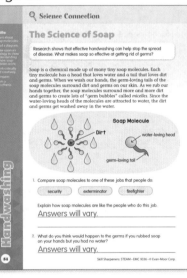

1. Compare soap molecules to one of these jobs that people do:
   security   exterminator   firefighter
   Explain how soap molecules are like the people who do this job.
   Answers will vary.

2. What do you think would happen to the germs if you rubbed soap on your hands but had no water?
   Answers will vary.

Page 85

Epidemiologists

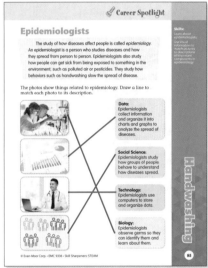

Page 91

Kylie's Problems

Answer the items about the story you read.

1. Each sentence states a problem in the story. Write numbers to rank the problems from 1 to 3, with 1 being the most difficult or serious problem in your opinion and 3 being the least difficult or serious problem.

   ☐ The way other people treat Kylie ruins her day and makes her feel lousy. Answers will vary.

   ☐ Kylie does not have a place or a way that feels safe for her to address issues with Mary.

   ☐ Kylie's ideas for her science project are not being considered.

2. Do you think Joaquin's actions in the story were helpful or harmful? Justify your opinion.
   Answers will vary.

3. How could the outcome of the story have been different if Mr. Levine had not gotten involved? Describe one idea.
   Answers will vary.

4. Write one thing Kylie could have done differently in the story.
   Answers will vary.

5. Who do you relate to most in the story: Mary, Joaquin, or Kylie? Why?
   Answers will vary.

Page 97

Using Social Media

Read about the social media platforms. Use the descriptions to think about how you could use each platform to brighten someone's day and try to make it better. Write one way you could do this for each platform, and be specific.

Platform	How to use it to make someone's day better
My Frames lets you share videos with others instantly!	Answers will vary.
RaiSeMe! helps you raise donations for a cause and also lets you invite your friends to raise money.	
With PetPlay, you can post photos and videos of your pet, and pets can "request" connections with other pet friends, with the help of their human family members, of course!	

Page 98

Facts and Figures on Bullying

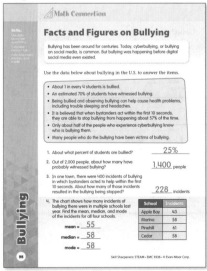

1. About what percent of students are bullied? **25%**
2. Out of 2,000 people, about how many have probably witnessed bullying? **1,400** people
3. In one town, there were 400 incidents of bullying in which bystanders acted to help within the first 10 seconds. About how many of those incidents resulted in the bullying being stopped? **228** incidents
4. The chart shows how many incidents of bullying there were in multiple schools last year. Find the mean, median, and mode of the incidents for all four schools.

School	Incidents
Apple Bay	43
Marina	58
Pinehill	61
Cedar	58

   mean __55__
   median __58__
   mode __58__

Page 99

People Who Work in the Field of SEL

Social and Emotional Learning (SEL) is a field of study that focuses on healthy and responsible ways to express emotions and deal with different situations. Many SEL experts are teachers. SEL experts can help people of all ages develop skills and also help people dealing with bullying. People who work as SEL professionals are able to practice SEL skills themselves.

You can learn more about what an SEL expert's work is about. Read about self-awareness and responsible decision making below. In the empty circles, write one sentence that tells how you have self-awareness and make responsible decisions.

knowing what you're good at · knowing what you can improve on · trying to understand what makes you feel emotions · Self-awareness · **Answers will vary.**

doing the right thing in tough situations · Responsible decision making · **Answers will vary.** · being honest · following safety rules

Bullying

© Evan-Moor Corp. • EMC 9336 • Skill Sharpeners: STEAM — 99

Page 105

What Now?

Answer the items about the story you read.

1. List three problems in the story.
   - Problem 1 **Answers will vary.**
   - Problem 2
   - Problem 3

2. How did the skate park benefit people in the town who didn't even skate?
   Answers will vary.

3. Draw two pictures of other activities Priya and her friends could have done other than watching TV. **Drawings will vary.**

4. List two possible consequences for the town or the characters in the story if the young skaters in the town never find another place to skate.
   - Consequence 1 **Answers will vary.**
   - Consequence 2

Nowhere to Skate

© Evan-Moor Corp. • EMC 9336 • Skill Sharpeners: STEAM — 105

Page 111

Skateboarding Physics

A skate park is designed especially for skateboarders, who often practice tricks and moves. In skateboard tricks like the ollie, the skateboard leaves the ground with the rider's feet. It looks as if the board is glued to the rider's feet, but, of course, it's not. Gravity keeps people and objects on the ground. It acts on the center of a person or object. By applying force to the back of the skateboard, a rider can make the front pop up. To get the back to lift up, the rider then applies pressure to the front.

Look at the photos. Then answer the items.

1. What do the positions of the skateboards have in common in both of the photos showing ollies? Explain why both boards are like this.
   Answers will vary.

2. Draw a picture of what would happen if a skateboarder tried to do an ollie but could not apply enough force to go against gravity.
   Drawings will vary.

Nowhere to Skate

© Evan-Moor Corp. • EMC 9336 • Skill Sharpeners: STEAM — 111

Page 112

Skate Park Construction

There are different kinds of skate parks. Some are outdoors and some are indoors. Some are meant to be permanent and some are set up just temporarily for a competition. Skate park designers build skate parks differently based on the location, their budget, and the park's purpose.

Look at the photos of skate parks being built. Then answer the items.

Park A · Park B

1. Compare and contrast the two skate parks shown. Write one thing in each part of the Venn diagram. **Answers will vary.**
   Park A · Both · Park B

2. Which skate park do you think costs less money to build? Which one do you think will stay in good condition for longer? Explain your thinking.
   Answers will vary.

Nowhere to Skate

Skill Sharpeners: STEAM • EMC 9336 • © Evan-Moor Corp. — 112

Page 113

Skateboard Business

Young skateboarders often dream of being professional skaters. Even if a person does not become a professional skateboarding athlete, he or she can still have a career in that field. Skateboarding magazines, videos, and websites are usually created by people who like to skate themselves. Other jobs in the field include owning a skateboard shop, designing art for skateboards, repairing boards, and designing skate parks.

Answer the items.

1. List six other jobs you can think of that a person might be able to do in the field of skateboarding that is not actually skateboarding.
   Answers will vary.

2. What is your favorite activity? Imagine that you aren't able to do it as a career, but you still want to work in that industry. Describe a job you could do in that industry and why you would like it.

My favorite activity	Job I could do
Answers will vary.	

Nowhere to Skate

© Evan-Moor Corp. • EMC 9336 • Skill Sharpeners: STEAM — 113

Page 119

Earning Money

Answer the items about the story you read.

1. Describe how one problem in the story causes another problem.
   Problem 1 **Answers will vary.** causes Problem 2

2. Explain how a loan could help Danso's family.
   Answers will vary.

3. Complete the sentence to compare how Danso's mother and father make money for the family.
   They both depend on **the environment** to make money for the family. This makes it challenging to make money because **of the drought**

4. Are there any problems with the solution that Danso came up with? Explain.
   Answers will vary.

Microfinance

© Evan-Moor Corp. • EMC 9336 • Skill Sharpeners: STEAM — 119

Page 125

Exchange Rates

Countries around the world use different types of money, or currency. When we loan money, it gets converted to whatever currency is used in a particular country. The conversion rate can vary daily.

The bar graph shows the conversions from $1.00 (one U.S. dollar) into the currency for different countries. Use the graph to answer the items.

Currency Exchange Rates

Amount of Currency Equal to $1.00 (U.S.) — Cedi (Ghana), Rupee (India), Loti (Lesotho), Real (Brazil), Shilling (Kenya), Dinar (Algeria)

1. Approximately how many Kenyan shillings are equal to $1.00 U.S.? **100**

2. About how many U.S. dollars would you have to pay if something costs 140 Indian rupees? **2**

3. Which country on the graph has currency that is closest in value to the U.S. dollar? **Brazil**
   Explain your reasoning. **Answers will vary.**

Microfinance

© Evan-Moor Corp. • EMC 9336 • Skill Sharpeners: STEAM — 125

Page 126

Technology and Microfinance

In many places, people who need money do not have access to a bank. However, modern technology enables people in remote areas to access loans.

Thanks to online microfinance sites, people can use their mobile phone to get a microloan.

1. Do you think technology has made it easier for people to donate money and get microloans? Explain your thinking.
   Answers will vary.

2. How do you think people got microloans in the past, before cellphones and the Internet? Write two ideas.
   Idea 1: **Answers will vary.**
   Idea 2:

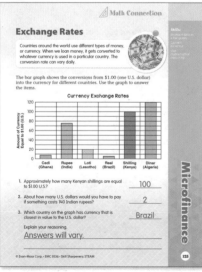

Microfinance

126 — © Evan-Moor Corp. • EMC 9336 • Skill Sharpeners: STEAM

Page 127

Starting a Business

People start businesses for different reasons. Many children have started their own businesses, too. There are certain things to decide on when starting a business. Read the descriptions and examples below. Then brainstorm ideas for two different businesses you would start if you could.

Name: What would the name of the business be?
Product or service: What would the business make or do to earn money?
Who: Who would you sell to? You could sell to children, adults, musicians, athletes, or other groups of people. Who would want to pay for your product or service?

Examples of products that a business could make:
bicycle parts · video games · exercise equipment · chairs

Examples of services that a business could provide:
washing cars · repairing skateboards · mowing lawns · cutting hair

Name: **Answers will vary.** · **Name:**
Product or service: · **Product or service:**
Who: · **Who:**

Microfinance

© Evan-Moor Corp. • EMC 9336 • Skill Sharpeners: STEAM — 127
